THE OPENING
AL-FATIHA

THE OPENING

AL-FATIHA

A Commentary on
the First Chapter of the Qur'an

M. Fethullah Gülen

NEW JERSEY • LONDON • FRANKFURT • CAIRO

TUGHRA
BOOKS
New Jersey

Originally published in Turkish as *Fatiha Üzerine Mülâhazalar* in 1997

19 18 17 16   1 2 3 4

Published by Tughra Books
335 Clifton Avenue, Clifton
New Jersey 07011, USA

www.tughrabooks.com

Library of Congress Cataloging-in-Publication Data
Names: Gülen, Fethullah, author.
Title: The opening (al-Fatiha) : a commentary on the first chapter of the
  Qurãan / M. Fethullah Gulen.
Other titles: Fatiha Üzerine mülahazalar. English
Description: Clifton, NJ : Tughra Books, 2016. | Includes bibliographical
  references.
Identifiers: LCCN 2016029962 | ISBN 9781597843928 (pbk.)
Subjects: LCSH: Qur'an. Surat al-Fatihah--Commentaries.
Classification: LCC BP128.16 .G8513 2016 | DDC 297.1/22721--dc23
LC record available at https://lccn.loc.gov/2016029962

ISBN: 978-1-59784-392-8

Printed in Canada by Marquis Book Printing.

Contents

Part Two
PRELUDE TO AL-FATIHA

Part Three
COMMENTARY ON THE VERSES

Preface

The Qur'an begins with the *surah* of Fatiha. The *surah* is also the beginning of *Salah*, Muslim's Daily Prayers. The doors to all good works can be opened with this diamond key, and all darkness in our life can be illumined with this source of light. In this respect, it is called *al-Fatiha* (the Opening) for it is the beginning of all goodness in life. It is also called *ash-Shafiya* (the Healer) for it cures many afflictions, material or spiritual, individual or social. It is called *al-Kafiya* (the Sufficient) for it is an adequate prescription for humanity's all needs and problems. It is called *Umm al-Kitab* (the Mother of the Book) for it is the summary of the Qur'anic truths and the index of all true books.

Fatiha is a blessed *surah* as comprehensive as a book. It contains the main purposes and principles of the Qur'an and all Holy Books. We can determine the essential subjects of the Qur'an as faith, worship, and morality or the order of life, and it is always possible to find in Fatiha an explicit or implicit reference, or at least a sign, to the aspects of these subjects. The principles of Islamic faith are not some abstract ideas. They are vital values which must be known, reflected upon, believed and internalized, and with which one should achieve the true submission to God. These vital values will be deepened with reflection and remembrance and nourished by worship in the broadest sense of the terms. If we consider them in our human relations and daily affairs, we will not be overcome by our desires and immoralities. In this way, a believer can stay in the sphere of faith all time, revolving around its main axis. All matters of faith and its practice are reflected in Fatiha in a great harmony.

Fatiha at first introduces God who is truly worthy of praise and gratitude. It introduces Him with some of His Attributes that are the essential wisdom behind creation. The *surah* emphasizes the fact that God has absolute authority over all things, drawing attention to our need of submission to this authority. Fatiha advises that we should seek help only from God in the face of all hardships and responsibilities that accompany this submission. It reminds us of the most important subject of help for humanity, which is our need of guidance. This need is presented in a striking image: the desirable way of those who have attained God's favors and blessings since the beginning and who have never known the misfortune of going astray.

Fatiha functions as the introduction of the Qur'an. The contents of all other *surah*s are summarized or implied in this very first chapter. The explanation of this fact can be found in corpuses of traditional Qur'anic exegesis and in part in this tiny volume.

This book was originally formed out of the lectures I gave to the public in the mosque. The content was not intended to form a book at all. As I addressed to the feelings and thoughts of the congregation, the spoken language determined the style for the most part even after the partial editing. The manner of preaching allowed some repetitions, which I could not eliminate completely from the text. There are only a few occasions where I could not avoid using technical language; but overall the text is quite plain and easy to read. The publication of this edition was not my idea. Some friends of mine initiated the project and I simply respected their initiative. I hope and pray it would be useful for the believers.

The Opening (Al-Fatiha)

In the Name of God, the All-Merciful, the All-Compassionate.

All praise is for God, the Lord of the worlds, the All-Merciful, the All-Compassionate, the Master of the Day of Judgment.

You alone do We worship, and from You alone do we seek help.

Guide us to the Straight Path, the Path of those whom You have favored, not of those who have incurred Your wrath, nor of those who are astray.

Amin.

Introduction

لَوْ أَنزَلْنَا هَذَا الْقُرْآنَ عَلَى جَبَلٍ لَّرَأَيْتَهُ خَاشِعاً مُّتَصَدِّعاً مِنْ

خَشْيَةِ اللهِ وَتِلْكَ الْأَمْثَالُ نَضْرِبُهَا لِلنَّاسِ لَعَلَّهُمْ يَتَفَكَّرُون

If We had sent down this Qur'an on a mountain, you would certainly
see it humble itself, splitting asunder for awe of God. Such parables
We strike for humankind so that they may reflect (al-Hashr 59:21).

T his verse explains that the Qur'an, the eternal word of God,
was sent to all people, who were created in the *"best form of
creation"* (at-Tin 95:4) and as capable for receiving the Divine
speech. If the Qur'an was sent down to the mountains instead of
humanity, one would see them shattered in pieces due to the greatness of this Divine revelation. The mountains would be so due to their
deep fear of God. Yet the Qur'an does not have such a deep impact on
the people who keep their hearts and minds from it. We cannot benefit from the Qur'an if we alienate our feelings from it and if we do not
reserve a special place for it in our hearts and minds.

> *The Qur'an is an ocean full of gems*
> *For the ones who can dive deep;*
> *But there can be no benefit from the Qur'an*
> *For the ones with no feel of need.*

God revealed the Qur'an with a profound capacity to respond to
all material and spiritual needs of humanity. In this sense, the Qur'an
is fully blessed and sacred. Its holiness and transcendence have no

match. It is purely Divine blessing. When people obey its command-ments, their lives become blessed and they rise above nations. All areas of life are rejuvenated with the merit of obedience to the Qur'an. Each field shoots forth and blooms, turning the earth into a paradise.

To reflect upon all these matters is the purpose of the revelation of the Qur'an. We should contemplate the Qur'an through a persistent intellectual activity and find its answers to the needs of our time. Other-wise, we cannot fully understand the Qur'an. In this regard, God says:

$$ كِتَابٌ أَنْزَلْنَاهُ إِلَيْكَ مُبَارَكٌ لِيَدَّبَّرُوا ءَايَاتِهِ وَلِيَتَذَكَّرَ أُولُو الْأَلْبَابِ $$

This is a Book, which We send down to you, full of blessings, so that they may ponder its verses, and that the people of discernment may reflect on it and be mindful (Sa'ad 38:29).

The word لِيَدَّبَّرُوا in the verse means to study and reflect upon some-thing in a diligent and thorough manner. The Qur'an should be stud-ied in this way. In addition, the phrase وَلِيَتَذَكَّرَ أُولُو الْأَلْبَابِ implies that the people of intelligence will discover further truths and penetrate sub-tler realities by the merit of studying the Qur'an.

The Qur'an reveals the truths manifestly. I cannot imagine a per-son who will seriously read the Qur'an but not take the path of God.

$$ أَفَلَا يَتَدَبَّرُونَ الْقُرْءَانَ أَمْ عَلَى قُلُوبٍ أَقْفَالُهَا $$

Do they not meditate earnestly on the Qur'an, or are there locks on the hearts? (Muhammad 47:24).

The Qur'an is the life of our lives. The goodness of our life depends on how much seriously we take the Qur'an as guidelines for our lives. A life far from the Qur'an is distant from total goodness. The life of a nation will suffer chaos and anarchy to the degree of its distance from the Qur'an.

The Messenger of God, peace and blessings be upon him, says: "The best of you is he who learns the Qur'an and then teaches it."[1] Namely, the best believers are those who study the Qur'an to learn its truths

---

[1] *Sahih al-Bukhari*, Fadail al-Qur'an, 21; *Sunan at-Tirmidhi*, Fadail al-Qur'an, 15.

and then teach them to others. If we want to be among the best, we need to work to understand the Qur'an and communicate this understanding to people around us. To this end, we need to read the Qur'anic commentaries and realize its elaborate teachings. Only in this way can we observe and protect the Qur'an. We cannot benefit from its light effectively if we have only a loose relation with it.

I will make a statement at this point—may the Qur'an excuse me—with my heart trembling: The Qur'an is jealous: It does not give anything to those who are not truly in love with it. If you love the Qur'an and turn to it with all your hearts, it will turn to you. But if you approach it inattentively, it will not reveal its secrets to you. The Qur'an reflects its lights to the loving hearts that turn to it wholly. If you do not read it and reflect upon its meaning, you will be deprived of its blessing light. The Prophet, peace and blessings be upon him, says concerning this:

> "The one who is proficient in the recitation of the Qur'an will be with the honorable and obedient scribes (angels); and he who recites the Qur'an with difficulty, doing his best to recite it in the best way possible, will have a double reward."[2]

One of the two rewards is for reciting the Qur'an, while the other is for the difficulty that would be faced by the untrained or handicapped. As the Qur'an is a Divine treasure, it is entirely good. If you recite it proficiently and in a way that befits its dignity, you will rise to the level of the angels. If you are a beginner and cannot recite it well, you will not be left destitute but rewarded twice instead.

The Messenger of God, peace and blessings be upon him, makes the following comment:

> "A believer who recites the Qur'an is like an orange whose fragrance is nice and taste is sweet. A believer who does not recite the Qur'an is like a date which has no fragrance but has a sweet taste. The hypocrite who recites the Qur'an is like the basil whose fragrance is nice but taste is bitter. A hypocrite who does not recite the Qur'an is like the colocynth which has no fragrance and has a bitter taste."[3]

---

[2]   *Sahih Muslim*, Salat al-Musafirin, 244; *Sunan Ibn Majah*, Adab, 52.
[3]   *Sahih al-Bukhari*, Fadail al-Qur'an, 17, 26; *Sahih Muslim*, Salat al-Musafirin, 37.

xvi The Opening (Al-Fatiha)

Comparing the believer who recites the Qur'an to an orange, the Prophet, peace and blessings be upon him, teaches us that the believer with a strong connection to the Qur'an will acquire a good life that gives good smell and flavor to the others. This beautiful effect actually originates in the believer's connection to God, a connection that is established by the Qur'an. In other words, the Qur'an governs the believer's life and directs it towards beautiful ends. This charming beauty radiates from the believer's person and has an impact on the surroundings. The following episode perfectly exemplifies this:

When Mecca could not shelter the believers anymore in its bosom because of the persecutions by the pagans, Abu Bakr, the closest companion of the Prophet, was among those oppressed. He once intended to migrate to Abyssinia just like many of his friends who had gone before. On his way, he came across one of the pagans, a moderate man named Ibn Daghinna. The latter asked him where he was heading to. Abu Bakr, may God be pleased with him, replied:

"My people have driven me out. They don't want me among them anymore."

Ibn Daghinna was upset and said:

"How could a man like you be driven out of Mecca? You support the poor and help the orphans and widows. Stay in the city under my protection."

Abu Bakr returned to Mecca and Ibn Daghinna announced his protection for him. This meant, according to the custom, that nobody could bother Abu Bakr anymore. He retired to his home where he enjoyed praying and reciting the Qur'an. All nights, he was praying near the window and his tearful recitation of the Qur'an was heard from outside. Many times people were gathering around his home to listen to his touching recitation. Upon this, the leaders of the pagans went to Ibn Daghinna and wanted him to stop protecting Abu Bakr. For solution, Ibn Daghinna demanded Abu Bakr not to recite the Qur'an. But he did not agree:

"How can I stop reciting the Qur'an when God reveals it to be proclaimed? You may cease to protect me, but I will continue to recite it under God's protection."[4]

The Qur'an is sweet as an orange. Whoever experiences its taste will fall in love with it. The Qur'an also has a scent. Whoever smells it will start to whirl around the sacred Book like a dervish in ecstasy. This is the position of true believers. The Qur'an finds its true meaning in their souls, hearts, and tongues.

As for the believer who does not recite the Qur'an, the Prophet, peace and blessings be upon him, compares him to a date, which has no fragrance but has a sweet taste. Although having experienced the taste of faith and benefitted from the revelation, such a believer does not have a great impact on his surroundings for he is not capable to spread the beautiful scent of the Qur'an around his community. Then the Qur'an remains confined or blocked. He is a believer, yet he limits the lights of the Qur'an that are meant to radiate. This is due to his failure in truly approaching the Qur'an and in fully realizing its graceful teachings.

As Muslims we are responsible for some duties towards the Qur'an. These duties are not limited to its preservation. We should respect to the content more than its container. A treasure deserves more attention than its chest. We will not fulfill the duty of respect towards the Qur'an when we place it on a nice shelf at our home. If you received a letter from the king, what would you do? Would you kiss it with respect and keep it in a special place without reading it? Or would you wonder what the king says, and immediately open it and read it carefully?

Here is a letter sent by God, the King of the kings. It is a letter so vital for you, for it addresses to the most important matters concerning this life and the next. If you kiss it and put it in a special place without paying attention to its content, can this attitude please the Authority who sent it to you? The Qur'an is a royal edict, a Divine letter sent to you as an honor and blessing in order that you may regulate your life meaningfully. God says in this letter:

---

4   *Sahih al-Bukhari*, Manaqib al-Ansar, 45.

وَلَقَدْ كَرَّمْنَا بَنِي ءَادَمَ

Assuredly We have honored the children of Adam (al-Isra 17:70).

This verse can be interpreted that God dignified us with the revelation of the Qur'an. We have been honored with the Qur'an specially. To respect truly the Qur'an is the way to receive this honor fully.

In a hadith, the Messenger of God, peace and blessings be upon him, says:

> "The one who recites the Qur'an aloud is like one who gives charity publicly. The one who recites the Qur'an in secret is like one who gives charity in secret."[5]

Just as charities are given publicly so that others will be encouraged to participate in this good deed, the Qur'an can be recited in public to encourage others to hold fast to their Book. On the other hand, being alone with the Qur'an, especially at nights, has another virtue that can be compared to the virtue of giving charity privately. In this privacy, we have a chance to search our own place in the Qur'an. It is very important for a believer to search a personal place in the Qur'an from which to direct his life. This kind of search is important because the quality of our faith depends on it. The great names of Islamic piety in the past—from Umar ibn Abd al-Aziz to Muhammad ibn Ka'b al-Qurazi—recited the Qur'an at nights in this manner and reached its true meanings and depths.

A sincere and beautiful recitation of the Qur'an will revitalize our souls, hearts, and feelings. Especially, listening to the Qur'an as if it is recited by the Prophet himself will enrapture us with infinite peace. Rising one degree above, listening to the Qur'an as if from the angelic person of Gabriel, the heavenly messenger of Divine revelation, will expose our soul to indescribable breezes of eternity. And beyond all, listening to the Qur'an as if we are the direct audience of its Eternal Speaker— even if I do not know whether a heart can endure this experience— will almost change our nature, making us into heavenly creatures.

---

5   *Sunan at-Tirmidhi*, Fadail al-Qur'an, 20; *Sunan Abu Dawud*, Tatawwu', 25; *Sunan an-Nasa'i*, Zakah, 6.

Part One

A Brief Journey to the Magical
World of the Qur'an

I.
Implications of the Word "Qur'an"

Arabic linguists agree that the word "Qur'an" means "recitation." They also argue that it may mean "collection" or bringing together things dispersed. These meanings can be interpreted in regard to the Qur'anic wisdom: The Qur'an is a thorough recitation or a complete collection of the truths which humanity could not attain without it. Except for this magnificent corpus of recited wisdom, people could not make judgments valid eternally regarding life and existence.

There is not a single matter of life and existence that is not explained or mentioned in the Qur'an. Concerning this quality of the Qur'an, God says:

مَا فَرَّطْنَا فِي الْكِتَابِ مِنْ شَيْءٍ

We have neglected nothing in the Book (al-An'am 6:38).

However, the Qur'an does not deal with all things in the same manner. Some of them are spoken of explicitly and some implicitly; some are explained completely while others pointed out with a sign. In this sense, the Qur'an is *an explanation of all things* (Yusuf 12:111) as described by itself.

وَلَا رَطْبٍ وَلَا يَابِسٍ إِلَّا فِي كِتَابٍ مُبِينٍ

Neither anything green nor dry, but is (recorded) in a manifest book (al-An'am 6:59).

Indeed, all things in creation, from atoms to celestial bodies, have a place in the Qur'an. But each finds its place according to its value and significance. There is a hierarchy of importance in the Qur'an, which reserves the highest rank for the matters of faith and morality but does not exclude any matters of less importance.

The Messenger of God, peace and blessings be upon him, says:

"Every verse has an explicit and an implicit meaning, and there is a limit for every recitation and interpretation."[6]

The Prophetic saying tells us that the Qur'anic verses reveal transcendent truths, some of which are manifest and some others subtle. The subtleties of the Qur'an are fully known only by God and may be discovered in part by those with profound knowledge (Al Imran 3:7). And each verse will be recited and interpreted according to some linguistic limits, which constitute the boundaries of meaning, either explicit or implicit.

Ja'far as-Sadiq, a prominent Muslim jurist and community leader of early Islam, says: "God manifests Himself to His servants in His speech that is the Qur'an, but most of them cannot see Him."[7] Indeed, God is manifest in the Qur'an, for the Qur'an is a mirror that reflects the meaning of the essential Divine qualities. God reveals the truth of His Attributes and works according to their transcendence and our capacity of understanding. The Qur'an is an interpreter of the Divine, in this sense. As we recite it in a proper manner, by giving each word its due and contemplating every verse, God will be revealed to our conscience. We will get closer to Him more and more, and finally we will feel united with Him.

The Qur'an represents humanity's true knowledge of God, for the Qur'an is where we meet God and unite with Him. We will know God according to the degree of our closeness to Him and we can get close to Him by the merit of understanding the Qur'an. As we know Him as richly and truly as He reveals in His speech, we will fully attain the

---

6   Abd ar-Razzaq, *Al-Musannaf*, III, 358; Abu Ya'la, *Al-Musnad*, IX, 278; Tabarani, *Al-Mu'jam al-Awsat*, I, 236.

7   Zarkashi, *Al-Burhan fi 'Ulum al-Qur'an*, I, 452.

eternal wisdom. When we recite the Qur'an genuinely, we will really feel God speaking to us. We will discern His transcendent Person in the speech, contemplate His Names, Attributes, and works, and know that it is God that is coming closer. At this final and perfect point, as stated in a hadith, God will be our eyes by which we see, our tongue by which we speak, our ears by which we hear, and our heart in which we attain eternal truths.[8] Then we will see and hear in God's Name and consider of everything in accordance with His will. Our heart will spread everywhere the truths of His divinity, which is the "Hidden Treasure," using the Sufi terms.

The Qur'an has another title: al-Furqan, which literally means the one that distinguishes. Furqan tells about differences: It distinguishes the Creator from the creation, showing the distinction between the Worshipped One and the worshipper. Man is not a creator, so we need to serve the Creator. We are expected to reach the horizon of perfect wisdom where we should discover the secrets of the Divine and recognize our place in between contingence and necessity. With this discovery and recognition, we will say, "I am not a god, but only a servant." Furqan signifies this humble position of ours. It signifies our human condition, the fact that we mix with fellow people and our sight is often veiled against the realm of the Divine. This is the lowest degree of what Furqan means. In the highest degree, we recognize the Divine unity at the face of the multiplicity of creation. This is the degree that we witness God by the eyes of all fellow creatures. It is to observe the manifestations of God's Attributes of glory and beauty in every part of the universe. With such an experience, a pantheist will say, "All is God." But we as the students of the Qur'an will say, "All is from God." With this, we express the highest degree of what Sufis call *farq*, the consciousness of "difference" between the Divine and the rest of existence.

We should endeavor to understand God in His own speech that is called both the Qur'an and Furqan. This endeavor will bring us to a level of consciousness that we will perceive the entire universe as a flowing scene of the Divine manifestations.

---

[8] For the hadith, see *Sahih al-Bukhari*, Riqaq, 38; Ahmad ibn Hanbal, *Al-Musnad*, VI, 256.

II.
The Qur'an: The Eternal Music

Recitation of the Qur'an has a musical quality. Although some Muslim jurists did not approve the Qur'an to be recited with singing voice, it is obvious that the Qur'anic verses have a poetic style that allows intonation or chanting. I believe that we need to approach the matter from the point of view that we naturally need to satisfy our sense of music in our soul. Such an approach will be more suitable to the spirit of a religion that considers every need of people.

It is narrated that the Messenger of God, peace and blessings be upon him, once passed by the house of Abu Musa al-Ash'ari, one of his companions, and heard his recitation of the Qur'an with a beautiful melodic voice. After listening to him for a while, he commended his recitation by comparing it to that of Prophet Dawud.[9] The Prophet, peace and blessings be upon him, encouraged people to recite the Qur'an sincerely, in a beautiful manner, and with a sweet voice, for such recitation would help others love the Qur'an and engage with it. In another hadith, God's Messenger is reported to have said: "Embellish the Qur'an with your voices."[10]

Ibn Mas'ud, may God be pleased with him, narrates:

The Messenger of God, peace and blessings be upon him, once said to me: "Recite the Qur'an to me." I said: "Shall I recite it to you although

---

[9] *Sahih al-Bukhari*, Fadail al-Qur'an, 31; *Sahih Muslim*, Salat al-Musafirin, 235–236.
[10] *Sunan an-Nasa'i*, Witr, 20; Iftitah, 83; *Sunan Ibn Majah*, Iqama, 176

it has been revealed to you?" He said: "I like listening to the Qur'an from others." So I recited the *surah* of an-Nisa till I reached the verse: *"How, then, will it be (with people on the Day of Judgment) when We bring forward a witness from every community and bring you (O Messenger) as a witness against these people?"* (an-Nisa 4:41). Then he said, "Stop." Behold, his eyes were shedding tears then.[11]

It was as if the verses Ibn Mas'ud recited made the Prophet exhausted. Perhaps, if Ibn Mas'ud had continued to recite a few more verses, the heart of the Prophet would have melted.

As the Messenger of God says, the Qur'an was revealed with sadness and should be recited with sadness.[12] For the Qur'an reveals humanity's serious condition on earth and our widespread lack of understanding. Man wanders in the middle of a wild desert called the world, with his limited power and resources. If he holds to the Qur'an, that "strong rope" in the Prophet's words, he will rise to the sky of true humanity. Freed from the suffocating air of this savage desert of loneliness, he will find a chance to be a perfect human. Our condition in the world is so serious, and the Qur'an makes us feel this fact when we read or recite it. For a deep feeling of this kind, one should delve into the depths of the meanings of the verses. Otherwise, it is impossible to feel the great impact of the Qur'an in our heart.

---

[11] *Sahih al-Bukhari*, Fadail al-Qur'an, 33, 35; *Sahih Muslim*, Salat al-Musafirin, 247–248

[12] Tabarani, *Al-Mu'jam al-Awsat*, III, 193; *Sunan Ibn Majah*, Iqamah, 176; Abu Ya'la, *Al-Musnad*, II, 50.

III.
The Collection and Preservation of the Qur'an

The first two generations of Islam, namely the Companions and those who succeeded them, were absolutely eager and earnest to learn the Qur'an. They could travel through deserts in order to get a single truth of it. An example is reported by Imam ash-Sha'bi. He tells that Masruq ibn al-Ajda, a well-known scholar of the second generation, was not sure of the interpretation of a Qur'anic verse. He traveled from Medina to Basra to ask a scholar of the meaning of the verse. The scholar told him he did not know the answer and referred him to another scholar in Damascus. Thereupon, Masruq set off to Damascus without delay.[13] Imagine how difficult it was that time to travel between those cities, when people had no other vehicles than camels or horses to cross a desert. Nonetheless, no hardship could not stop a noble man like Masruq from traveling from city to city to chase after a better interpretation of a single verse.

Another scholar of the second generation, Ikrima, the student of the renowned companion Ibn Abbas, tells that he searched for fourteen years for the name of the person who was described in the verse:

13 Abu Nu'aym, *Hilya al-Awliya*, II, 95; Ibn Asakir, *Tarikh Dimashq*, LVII, 397.

وَمَنْ يَخْرُجْ مِنْ بَيْتِهِ مُهَاجِرًا إِلَى اللهِ وَرَسُولِهِ ثُمَّ يُدْرِكْهُ

الْمَوْتُ فَقَدْ وَقَعَ أَجْرُهُ عَلَى اللهِ

He who leaves his home as an emigrant to God and His Messenger, and whom death overtakes (while still on the way), his reward is due and sure with God (an-Nisa 4:100).

Who was this man whose name was not mentioned in the verse? Why did Ikrima spend this much effort to clarify his identity? Perhaps he thought that this person's place in the community and his character would shed light to the interpretation of the verse. Ikrima kept searching for years and at last he learned that the person was Damra ibn Jundub, who attempted to migrate from Mecca to Medina in God's cause but died on the way from illness.[14]

Similarly, Ibn Abbas, may God be pleased with him, says that he was curious about the two wives of the Prophet, peace and blessings be upon him, mentioned in the following verse:

إِنْ تَتُوبَا إِلَى اللهِ فَقَدْ صَغَتْ قُلُوبُكُمَا وَإِنْ تَظَاهَرَا عَلَيْهِ فَإِنَّ اللهَ هُوَ

مَوْلَاهُ وَجِبْرِيلُ وَصَالِحُ الْمُؤْمِنِينَ وَالْمَلَائِكَةُ بَعْدَ ذَلِكَ ظَهِيرٌ

If you two turn to God in repentance (then that is indeed what you should do); for the hearts of both of you swerved (from what is right). But if you back each other up against him, God Himself is his Guardian, and that Gabriel, and the righteous ones among the believers, and all the angels besides, are his helpers (at-Tahrim 66:4).

The verse was talking about the Prophet's two wives who once together offended their husband regarding a family matter. But who were these wives? Ibn Abbas says that he thought Umar ibn al-Khattab, the caliph of the time and a close friend of the Prophet, looked the best person to ask. However, he waited for a long time to ask Umar of this matter because Umar was a man of majesty. At last he found a chance and

---

[14] Ibn Abd al-Barr, *Al-Isti'ab*, II, 750; Abu Hayyan, *Al-Bahr al-Muhit*, III, 350.

asked him. Umar told him that they were Aisha and Hafsa, may God be pleased with them.[15]

We can give hundreds of examples of this kind which would prove that the earliest generations of Islam were absolutely serious about the knowledge of the Qur'an and that they could tirelessly seek after a single truth of it for weeks or months, or even years. And the Companions were the first generation who took all pains to keep and preserve the authentic recitation and interpretation of the Qur'an.

The Qur'an was revealed in twenty three years. The Prophet, peace and blessings be upon him, had scribes from his companions whom he dictated the verses upon their revelation. The scribes used primitive materials to write on such as flat bones, pieces of wood or animal skin. In addition, there were many *hafiz*s at that time, who were to memorize every revealed part of the Qur'an and hence the entire Scripture. Ibn Mas'ud, Zayd ibn Thabit, Ubay ibn Ka'b, Uthman ibn Afwan, and hundreds of others, may God be pleased with them, knew the entire Qur'an by heart.[16] When a verse was revealed, God's Messenger, peace and blessings be upon him, indicated its place in its particular chapter based on the revelation. The *hafiz*s followed this instruction in their memorization. The chapters of the Qur'an were again sorted according to the revelation.[17] In short, the revelation was preserved immediately by the merit of professional recording and memorization.

After the death of the Prophet, many *hafiz*s died in the battle of Yamama. This worried Umar ibn al-Khattab may God be pleased with him, and caused him to talk to the caliph Abu Bakr may God be pleased with him. Umar said to him that the loss of *hafiz*s in battles was a serious problem for the learning and preservation of the Qur'an. He suggested convening the *hafiz*s and bringing the written materials together in order to compile the Qur'an in a single volume. Abu Bakr hesitated at first because this was a thing that the Prophet, peace and blessings be upon him, neither did nor advised to be done after him. Umar con-

[15] *Sahih Muslim*, Talaq, 30; *Sunan an-Nasa'i*, Siyam, 14; Ahmad ibn Hanbal, *Al-Musnad*, I, 33.
[16] See *Sahih al-Bukhari*, Fadail al-Qur'an, 8; Ibn Hajar, *Fath al-Bari*, IX, 48–52
[17] *Sunan at-Tirmidhi*, Tafsir *surah* 9, 1; Ahmad ibn Hanbal, *Al-Musnad*, I, 57.

tinued to explain the matter and how important it was to have a compiled copy of the Qur'an. The caliph was finally convinced. They both agreed upon Zayd ibn Thabit, a *hafiz* and one of the scribes of the Prophet, to be the chief of a committee to work on the compilation. Zayd's initial response was almost identical to the caliph's. But he too was convinced and understood the significance of the task. The committee convened and started to collect all written materials to put them together according to the memorized order of the chapters and verses. The codex of the Qur'an was thus formed. The task was done by the clear agreement and confidence of all the members of the committee and rest of the community.

Even after this codification, the Qur'an was still to allow different ways of recitation to a certain extent based on the different Arabic dialects. In fact, the Prophet, peace and blessings be upon him, had allowed this plurality and explained that the Qur'an had been revealed according to several dialects.[18] Nonetheless, during the years of the third caliph, Uthman ibn Afwan, may God be pleased with him, the variations in the recitation of the same text caused some sort of disagreements among the people. Worried by these disagreements, Hudhayfa ibn al-Yaman, a renowned Companion and an officer at the time, applied to Uthman and suggested making multiple copies of the Qur'an and distributing them to the central cities of the country to let people follow the same text for their recitation. Then the caliph commissioned a committee for the purpose that was formed of *hafiz*s and scribes. The committee worked diligently to unify the Qur'anic text into a single script according to the central dialect of Arabic of the time and make seven exact copies of it. This was about twenty years after the death of the Prophet. The copies were sent to different cities as authoritative codices of the Qur'an.[19]

From that time on, the Qur'an has been preserved as exactly the same. Throughout the Islamic history, there has been only one version of the Qur'an in the Muslim world. In fact, this is the fulfillment of the Divine promise given in the verse:

---

[18] *Sahih al-Bukhari*, Fadail al-Qur'an, 27; *Sahih Muslim*, Salat al-Musafirin, 270.

[19] See *Sahih al-Bukhari*, Fadail al-Qur'an, 3; Zurqani, *Manahil al-Irfan*, I, 181.

إِنَّا نَحْنُ نَزَّلْنَا الذِّكْرَ وَإِنَّا لَهُ لَحَافِظُونَ

Indeed it is We, We Who send down the Reminder in parts, and it is indeed We Who are its Guardian (al-Hijr 15:9).

God will protect the Qur'an until the Day of Judgment. If we hold fast to the Qur'an, it will be protected with us. If we hold fast to the Qur'an, our homes and country will be illumined with its light. If we can truly hold to it, we can attain the honor of being held dear by humanity.

IV.
The Qur'an as the Word of God

God speaks. Speech is one of His eternal Attributes. God created the universe and spoke to us about the universe and ourselves. In His last revelation, He speaks to us of His own Person, Attributes, and Names. He expounds His art work that is called human being, revealing the secrets of this mysterious creature. But God's speech is transcendent, so we are not capable to comprehend its essence. The Qur'an is formed of this transcendent speech. We see letters, words, and sentences in this speech, in its embodied form as Scripture, or we hear those words when recited. This embodiment is called the "uttered speech" (*al-kalam al-lafzi*) by theologians, a speech that is expressed in words or written with script. This is the manifestation of the Divine speech in the realm of humanity. On the other hand, the "inner speech" (*al-kalam an-nafsi*) does not denote such materialization and is used by theologians to refer to God's transcendent act of speech.

God's eternal speech should be conceived in transcendent sense and the concept of "internal speech" should remain a comparison for this conception. God eternally speaks, and the creation of the universe or our human existence cannot limit its time. In this sense, the Qur'an too is eternal, pre-existing the universe. Let me try to explain this subtle issue. When we recite or listen to the Qur'an, we understand God's "internal speech" in its physical manifestation. In other words, the transcendent Divine speech comes into existence at the same time that we utter the Qur'anic words. We feel the Divine quality of the speech even though it is we that express the words. God's "internal speech" enables us to recite the same Qur'anic *surahs* over and again without any feeling of boredom, even if we may be so familiar with the words themselves. We sense God's "internal speech" in the Qur'an but cannot comprehend it. We cannot determine its essence, just as our wisdom about the essence of Divine revelation does not go beyond our wonder. We can neither comprehend the transcendent quality of God's speech nor describe our spiritual pleasure originating from that quality.

In respect to this understanding, it is not correct to say, like Mu'tazili theologians: "The fact that God speaks means that God creates words." It is not correct, either, to say, like Kharijis and others: "God's speech consists of letters and sounds." These statements are meaningless. Although our recitation of the Qur'an is obviously contingent and created by God, this human practice is not the essence of the Divine speech. Its essence is eternal and can only be sensed in a spiritual manner in the recitation.

V.
The Qur'an as a Miracle

The Qur'an is a miracle. In Islamic terminology, "miracle" (*mu'jiza* in Arabic) means an extraordinary event created by God by the hand of His Prophet in order to prove his Prophethood. If a person claims to be God's Messenger, people will expect extraordinary things from him as a sign of his special capacity. If this person shows such unnatural things in the Name of God, we call them miracles. To consider an event a miracle, it must be really extraordinary, an event that can be generated only by Divine power, and must coincide and be suitable with the claim of Prophethood. Therefore, unusual acts of saints or phenomenal events are not to be called miracle in Islamic terminology.

The Qur'an has challenged humanity for centuries, proclaiming:

وَإِنْ كُنْتُمْ فِي رَيْبٍ مِمَّا نَزَّلْنَا عَلَى عَبْدِنَا فَأْتُوا بِسُورَةٍ مِنْ مِثْلِهِ وَادْعُوا شُهَدَاءَكُمْ مِنْ دُونِ اللهِ إِنْ كُنْتُمْ صَادِقِينَ

If you are in doubt about the Divine authorship of what We have been sending down on Our servant (Muhammad), then produce just a *surah* like it and call for help from all your supporters, all those to whom you apply for help apart from God, if you are truthful in your doubt and claim (al-Baqarah 2:23).

Nevertheless, humanity could never do such a thing and will never be able to do so. For the Qur'an is a miraculous word of God.

Let us now see the main aspects of the Qur'anic miracle in a brief way:

First of all, the style of the Qur'an is miraculous. It has a peculiar style, one that cannot be compared to any others. The Qur'an is poetic but not a poem; something in between poetry and prose. When the people of the time of its revelation listened to it, they found it really unusual, but they did not attribute to it any defects or flaws. It was utterly perfect in its use of Arabic language, so perfect that it would become the single greatest authority in Arabic grammar, vocabulary, and semantics. It was conventional in grammatical terms, but emerged with a completely new way of expression.

Secondly, the content of the Qur'an is miraculous. The Qur'an provides knowledge about metaphysical, natural, and historical realities, and puts forward spiritual, moral, and judicial judgments; all these in outstanding originality and consistency. It is not possible for a man or a group of people to know all these things and bring them together in such a harmonious way.

Thirdly, the composition of the Qur'an is miraculous. Even though it was gradually and occasionally revealed in twenty three years, answering countless questions and addressing to numerous issues, it has an eloquent and coherent flow that as if it was revealed at once to answer one question or to address to a single issue. The following verse talks about this Qur'anic harmony:

أَفَلَا يَتَدَبَّرُونَ الْقُرْءَانَ وَلَوْ كَانَ مِنْ عِنْدِ غَيْرِ اللَّهِ لَوَجَدُوا فِيهِ اخْتِلَافًا كَثِيرًا

Do they not contemplate the Qur'an? Had it been from any other than God, they would surely have found in it much incoherence and inconsistency (an-Nisa 4:82).

Some theologians claimed that people are not able to bring anything similar to the Qur'an because God prevents them to do so. This opinion, called *sarfa* or "prevention," does not seem to be correct. My heart does not tend to accept it. On the contrary, God allows people as He challenges them, but the miraculous quality of the Qur'an is out of reach for humanity. People could not imitate its words in the past, nor can they do in the future.

VI.
Definitions of the Qur'an

The Qur'an has many characteristics and it functions in many ways in our life. Below are some of the definitions of the Qur'an based on some of these characteristics and functions.

I. Interpretation of the Book of the Universe

The Qur'an interprets the great book of the universe. The universe is a book with its lines and pages organized in a perfect order, and there has to be a reader who will examine this book. The reader is humanity. But we need an adequate interpretation of this book to fully understand the intentions of its Author. To this end, God granted us, out of His mercy, the Qur'an as a perfect interpretation of His creation. We can learn the great truths of existence from the Qur'an, the truths that we are typically not able to discern directly in the face of the universe. Only the Creator can ensure us of the ultimate truths of all these natural phenomena, for the universe is God's making just as humanity is. The Qur'an is His speech about these two Divine works. So there is a profound relationship among the universe, humanity, and the Qur'an.

God Almighty says concerning this:

سَنُرِيهِمْ ءَايَاتِنَا فِي الْآفَاقِ وَفِي أَنْفُسِهِمْ حَتَّى يَتَبَيَّنَ لَهُمْ أَنَّهُ الْحَقُّ
أَوَلَمْ يَكْفِ بِرَبِّكَ أَنَّهُ عَلَى كُلِّ شَيْءٍ شَهِيدٌ

We will show them Our manifest signs in the horizons of the universe and within their own selves, until it will become manifest to them that it (the Qur'an) is indeed the truth. Is it not sufficient (as proof) that your Lord is a witness over all things? (Fussilat 41:53).

This verse teaches that all studies of natural and human sciences will show us signs that testify to the truths expressed in the Qur'an. Scientific studies will show us that the universe is a perfect and purposeful work of the Creator and that there is an eternal wisdom behind the human existence.

The laws of nature are God's signs (*ayat*) in creation. Howsoever these laws are formulated in natural sciences, these formulations will not change the ultimate meaning of the laws. They are signs indicating God's perfect will, power, and knowledge, as the following verse tells us:

إِنَّ فِي خَلْقِ السَّمَوَاتِ وَالْأَرْضِ وَاخْتِلَافِ اللَّيْلِ

وَالنَّهَارِ لَآيَاتٍ لِأُولِي الْأَلْبَابِ

Surely in the creation of the heavens and the earth, and the alternation of night and day, there are signs for the people of discernment (Al Imran 3:190).

The Qur'an interprets the signs of creation. It stands before the universe and introduces it to us, not only with its ultimate reality, but also its natural reality as well. Let us see some examples of this Qur'anic introduction.

The miracle of milk

وَإِنَّ لَكُمْ فِي الْأَنْعَامِ لَعِبْرَةً نُسْقِيكُمْ مِمَّا فِي بُطُونِهِ مِنْ بَيْنِ

فَرْثٍ وَدَمٍ لَبَنًا خَالِصًا سَائِغًا لِلشَّارِبِينَ

And surely in the cattle, there is a lesson for you: We give you from that which is within their bodies, (distinguished from) between the waste and blood, milk that is pure and palatable to those who drink (an-Nahl 16:66).

The food we consume is digested in our mouth and stomach, and most of the nutrients are absorbed through small intestine. These nutrients are absorbed by the capillaries and then used by the mammary glands for the production of milk. When we look at the verse in the light of this scientific information, we can understand that the verse refers to the refinement process of the milk, which takes place first in small intestine full of "waste" and then secondly out of "blood" in mammary glands. Normally, a matter that comes out of waste is discomforting. To eliminate this discomfort, the Qur'an uses the word "pure" as a quality of the milk. Again, something mixed with blood is not a good thing to drink. Against this notion, the verse describes the milk as "palatable." Obviously, these contrasts are mentioned by the Qur'an to indicate the miraculous production of milk.

Prophet Muhammad, peace and blessings be upon him, was unlettered, a historical fact that all Muslim and non-Muslim scholars alike agree upon. But a verse we listen to from him perfectly explains the nature of the production of milk. Even this single example is a proof clear enough for the unprejudiced people to recognize the Divine origin of the Qur'an.

Oxygen decreasing with elevation

فَمَنْ يُرِدِ اللهُ أَنْ يَهْدِيَهُ يَشْرَحْ صَدْرَهُ لِلْإِسْلَام وَمَنْ يُرِدْ أَنْ يُضِلَّهُ
يَجْعَلْ صَدْرَهُ ضَيِّقًا حَرَجًا كَأَنَّمَا يَصَّعَّدُ فِي السَّمَاءِ كَذَلِكَ
يَجْعَلُ اللهُ الرِّجْسَ عَلَى الَّذِينَ لَا يُؤْمِنُونَ

Whomever God wills to guide, He expands his breast to Islam, and whomever He wills to lead astray, He causes his breast to become tight and constricted, as if he were climbing towards the heaven. Thus, God lays ignominy upon those who do not believe (despite many signs and evidences) (al-An'am 6:125).

There is a comparison in the verse: The mood of an unbeliever is compared to the distress and anxiety that one feels when climbing towards the sky. The point of similarity is clear: We typically feel uneasy when climbing up to the sky. But this may also refer to the fact that we feel constriction in the lungs when ascending to the sky because the amount of oxygen in atmosphere decreases with elevation. This is a scientific fact that was unknown until the modern period. The Qur'an seems to refer to this fact in an implicit way. With this implication, the Qur'an seems also to draw our attention to the depressions and crises caused by unbelief in modern times.

Creation of everything in pairs

وَمِنْ كُلِّ شَيْءٍ خَلَقْنَا زَوْجَيْنِ لَعَلَّكُمْ تَذَكَّرُونَ

And all things We have created in pairs, so that you may reflect and be mindful (adh-Dhariyat 51:49).

In Arabic, if the word كُلّ ("every" or "all") modifies a noun without definite article, as it is the case in this verse, it refers to all members of the concept. The noun or concept here is شَيْءٍ which means "thing" and it applies to all creatures, living or not, in the universe. The word زَوْجَيْنِ means a pair or a couple. The verse tells that all creatures are created in pairs, referring to a universal reality in nature. Just as we humans have two genders, so do all animals and plants. There are two electric charges and two magnetic poles, and even the subatomic particles are said to have their respective couples. The following verse reveals this truth:

سُبْحَانَ الَّذِي خَلَقَ الْأَزْوَاجَ كُلَّهَا مِمَّا تُنْبِتُ
الْأَرْضُ وَمِنْ أَنْفُسِهِمْ وَمِمَّا لَا يَعْلَمُونَ

All-Glorified is He, Who has created the pairs all together out of what the earth produces, as well as out of (people) themselves, and out of what they do not know (Ya-Sin 36:36).

This verse clearly tells that there are much more things created in pairs that the people of the time of the revelation did not know. The verse also means that there are many things created in pairs that humanity in general do not know. We do not know how much more the scientific study will reveal to us in regard to this universal reality.

The atomic world

$$لَا يَعْزُبُ عَنْهُ مِثْقَالُ ذَرَّةٍ فِي السَّمَوَاتِ وَلَا فِي الْأَرْضِ وَلَا$$

$$أَصْغَرُ مِنْ ذَلِكَ وَلَا أَكْبَرُ إِلَّا فِي كِتَابٍ مُبِينٍ$$

Not an atom's weight of whatever there is in the heavens or in the earth escapes Him, nor is there anything smaller than that, or greater, but it is (recorded) in a Manifest Book (Saba 34:3).

This verse apparently tells that nothing is excluded from God's infinite knowledge and all-encompassing authority. From the realm of sub-atomic particles to that of nebulae and galaxies, everything is under God's control. This is the apparent meaning of the verse. But beyond this, it seems to refer to some subtle realities which have been revealed by modern scientific discoveries. First of all, the word ذَرَّة means the smallest part of matter. This word refers to tiny particles of dust or similar things in classical Arabic, as it was in the time of the revelation, and it came to be used to refer to the atom in modern period. Based on the essential meaning of the word, the verse can be said to refer implicitly to some atomic phenomena: atomic weight; something "smaller" than the atom, namely subatomic particles like electron; and something "greater" than the atom, namely molecules. None of these are excluded from God's knowledge and authority.

The beginning of the *surah* of adh-Dhariyat seems to have similar implications. Let us see these verses one by one:

$$وَالذَّارِيَاتِ ذَرْوًا$$

By those that (like winds) scatter far and wide (adh-Dhariyat 51:1).

The verse allows alternative translations as the first word can be interpreted by various ways. Literally, the word is associated with the dust clouds arisen by strong winds. Likewise, in an implicit way, the verse may refer to the electrons and their movements. As they move around the atomic nucleus so fast, electrons form a cloud-like structure.

$$فَالْحَامِلَاتِ وِقْرًا$$

And those that bear heavy burdens (adh-Dhariyat 51:2).

This vague phrase, too, allows alternative interpretations. Following the above commentary, this verse may refer implicitly to protons: they are heavy and play a central role in the formation of matter.

$$فَالْجَارِيَاتِ يُسْرًا$$

And those that run with gentle ease (adh-Dhariyat 51:3).

Finally, this verse seems to make an implicit reference to neutrons. Having no electric charge, these particles move freely and can run through, for example, a very thick lead plate easily.

The event of precipitation

$$وَأَرْسَلْنَا الرِّيَاحَ لَوَاقِحَ فَأَنْزَلْنَا مِنَ السَّمَاءِ مَاءً فَأَسْقَيْنَاكُمُوهُ وَمَا أَنْتُمْ لَهُ بِخَازِنِينَ$$

We send the winds to fertilize, and so We send down water from the sky, and give it to you to drink; it is not you who are the keepers of its stores (under earth) (al-Hijr 15:22).

There are many benefits of winds, and the verse mentions their role in the event of precipitation. The rest of the verse provides evidence that the "fertilization" does not refer to the well-known fact that plants are pollinated by the means of winds. It should refer to another phenomenon that is functional in the realization of precipitation. Another verse is more informative about the matter:

$$أَلَمْ تَرَ أَنَّ اللهَ يُزْجِي سَحَابًا ثُمَّ يُؤَلِّفُ بَيْنَهُ ثُمَّ يَجْعَلُهُ رُكَامًا فَتَرَى الْوَدْقَ$$

$$يَخْرُجُ مِنْ خِلَالِهِ وَيُنَزِّلُ مِنَ السَّمَاءِ مِنْ جِبَالٍ فِيهَا مِنْ بَرَدٍ فَيُصِيبُ بِهِ مَنْ$$

$$يَشَاءُ وَيَصْرِفُهُ عَنْ مَنْ يَشَاءُ يَكَادُ سَنَا بَرْقِهِ يَذْهَبُ بِالْأَبْصَارِ$$

Do you not see that God gently drives the clouds, then joins them together, and then turns them into a thick mass, and consequently you see rain-drops issue out of their midst. He sends down hail out of snow-laden mountains (of clouds) from the sky, and smites with it whom He wills, and averts it from whom He wills. The flash of the lightning almost takes away the sight (an-Nur 24:43).

The phrase "gently drives" refers to the function of winds to move the clouds in atmosphere smoothly. Then the verse tells how the clouds come together to form huge masses for the purpose of precipitation. Here we can consider the clouds with opposite electric charges to be brought together or "fertilized" by winds for the purpose of rainfall. In addition, the verse talks about the place where the raindrops are formed and from where they start to fall. It is interesting that the verse distinguishes this place from that of hail. We know that hail is formed at the top of the clouds which really look like "mountains" in the sky.

Expansion of the sky

وَالسَّمَاءَ بَنَيْنَاهَا بِأَيْدٍ وَإِنَّا لَمُوسِعُونَ

And the heaven, We have constructed it mightily; and it is surely We Who have vast power, and keep expanding it (adh-Dhariyat 51:47).

In Arabic, verb clauses denote renewal while noun clauses denote continuity. The second part of the verse is a noun clause in its original Arabic, and it denotes the continuity of the act of "expanding" in all times. In other words, it does not say, "We expanded it," or "We are expanding it." But it says, with a more precise translation: "We are the One who always expands it."

In 1922, Edwin Hubble announced that the galaxies are moving further away with speeds proportionate to their distances from the earth. This meant the expansion of the universe, an idea that was suggested earlier by the Belgian priest, mathematician, and astronomer George Lemaitre. The expansion of space has been widely accepted as a scientific fact, and it was pointed out by the Qur'an fourteen centuries ago.

Creation of the earth as a globe

خَلَقَ السَّمَوَاتِ وَالْأَرْضَ بِالْحَقِّ يُكَوِّرُ اللَّيْلَ عَلَى

النَّهَارِ وَيُكَوِّرُ النَّهَارَ عَلَى اللَّيْلِ

He has created the heavens and the earth with truth. He wraps the night around the day, and He wraps the day around the night (az-Zumar 39:5).

The earth is in the shape of a globe flattened a little from the poles. In Arabic, the verb used in the verse to define the Divine act of "wrapping" the night and day around each other essentially denotes to wrap something around a round thing, like turban cloth around the head. That is, the word "wrapping around" in the verse clearly indicates the global shape of the earth. Another verse points out to the same fact:

$$\text{وَالْأَرْضَ بَعْدَ ذَلِكَ دَحَاهَا}$$

> And after that He has spread out the earth in the egg-shape (for habitability) (an-Naziat 79:30).

Separation of the heavens and earth

$$\text{أَوَلَمْ يَرَ الَّذِينَ كَفَرُوا أَنَّ السَّمَوَاتِ وَالْأَرْضَ كَانَتَا رَتْقًا فَفَتَقْنَاهُمَا}$$

> Do those who disbelieve ever consider that the heavens and the earth were at first one piece, and then We parted them as separate entities? (al-Anbiya 21:30).

There are numerous galaxies and nebulas in the space with various types and shapes. God creates stars out of nebulas. Perhaps our solar system was a nebula, out of which God formed in time the sun and the planets, employing physical forces He determines like the gravitational and centrifugal ones. The verse seems to indicate this cosmological event: the creation of the solar system out of a single body. In fact, the word رَتْقًا (one piece) etymologically denotes a whole that is liquid or a sticky, cohering substance. God processed this whole or substance and created two separate yet relative entities called the earth and sky.

The "disbeliever" (*kafir*) means one who lies to his conscience, who misuses his physical and spiritual abilities, and who contradicts with his own heart. With the phrase "those who disbelieve," the verse does not only refer to the Meccan pagans, who had never stepped out of the desert and who knew the stars only by their bare eyes, but also the disbelievers of our modern times. The above verse in fact would not mean much to the ancient people in terms of cosmic history, at least, not as much as it means to the people of this age of scientific discoveries.

Creation of life out of water

$$\text{وَجَعَلْنَا مِنَ الْمَاءِ كُلَّ شَيْءٍ حَيٍّ}$$

We have made every living thing from water (al-Anbiya 21:30).

Water is the most essential element in all living bodies from the smallest cells to the giant sequoias. We cannot imagine life without water. With God's will, life emerged and developed in water on earth. The verse explicitly indicates this biological fact.

All these examples confirm the aforementioned truth that God Almighty has made the universe speak of its Maker by the language of the "signs" in it, and that He has made the Qur'an interpret these signs by its own language.

2. The Key of the Treasures of the Divine Names

The Qur'an interprets the Divine "signs" in creation and ultimately reveals the truths of the Divine Names that are reflected in both natural and human existence. What Divine Names are reflected in this and that phenomena? What Divine Names lie behind such and such events in the world? As the interpreter of the book of the universe, the Qur'an answers these questions by revealing the metaphysical nature of each reality. The Qur'an explains all phenomena with references to Divine Names, from the meaningful emergence of everything in the universe to the default purity of nature, to life that remains mysterious despite all curiosity and research.

$$\text{هُوَ اللهُ الَّذِي لَا إِلَهَ إِلَّا هُوَ عَالِمُ الْغَيْبِ وَالشَّهَادَةِ هُوَ الرَّحْمَنُ الرَّحِيمُ}$$

God is He save Whom there is no deity: the Knower of the unseen and the witnessed. He is the All-Merciful, the All-Compassionate (al-Hashr 59:22).

Our human existence has aspects related to the known and unknown, seen and unseen dimensions of the universal reality. Only the One who knows all aspects of our existence can sustain it. We all creatures need to be taken care of by the Divine Names "the All-Merciful" and "the All-Compassionate." We observe this universal care in all natural phenomena, in the infants nourished in the womb, in the plants nurtured in hard conditions.

هُوَ اللهُ الَّذِي لَا إِلَهَ إِلَّا هُوَ الْمَلِكُ الْقُدُّوسُ السَّلَامُ الْمُؤْمِنُ الْمُهَيْمِنُ

الْعَزِيزُ الْجَبَّارُ الْمُتَكَبِّرُ سُبْحَانَ اللهِ عَمَّا يُشْرِكُونَ

God is He save Whom there is no deity: the Sovereign, the All-Holy and the All-Pure, the Supreme Author of peace and salvation, and the Supreme Author of safety and security Who bestows faith and removes all doubt, the All-Watchful Guardian, the All-Glorious with irresistible might, the All-Compelling of supreme majesty, the One Who has exclusive right to all greatness. All-Glorified is God in that He is absolutely exalted above what they associate with Him (al-Hashr 59:23).

The Divine Name "Malik" (Sovereign) tells that God has an absolute authority in the universe. Due to the manifestations of His Name "Quddus" (All-Pure), nature is always purified from kinds of waste. The Qur'an explains this law of purification with reference to this Divine Name. Likewise, the Qur'an refers to the Name "Salam" (Peace) in respect to the general peace and security that we observe in the universe. Despite the apparent struggle among creatures, plants help animals survive just as animals help us live. In this central position, we seem to have signed an agreement with the entire universe. With His Name "Mu'min" (Source of Trust and Security), God has established safety and security in society, placing trust and confidence among its members.

In this way, we learn from the interpretation of the Qur'an the ultimate explanation of phenomena around us. We learn what Divine Names provide the wisdom behind what events in the universe.

3. Interpreter of the Divine Attributes

The Qur'an provides us with sufficient information about God's transcendent Person and Attributes. This rich information is everywhere in the Qur'an. To mention an example:

وَلَمْ يَكُنْ لَهُ كُفُوًا أَحَدٌ ۞ لَمْ يَلِدْ وَلَمْ يُولَدْ ۞ اللهُ الصَّمَدُ ۞ قُلْ هُوَ اللهُ أَحَدٌ

Say: He is God, the Unique One of Absolute Oneness. God is He Who is the Eternally-Besought-of-All. He begets not, nor is He begotten. And comparable to Him there is none (al-Ikhlas 112:1–4).

These verses, comprising a short *surah* in the Qur'an, teaches that God is one and unique. He is not in need of anything, but everything is in need of Him. The order of the universe is sustained by Him and relies upon His bestowal of existence. Humanity, too, needs Him in its all affairs. We could not survive on earth except for His providence. Absolutely transcendent, God is neither like men nor has offspring among them, and He never has an associate or partner.

With these few short statements, the Qur'an teaches us the most significant truths about divinity. Without this Qur'anic teaching, we might follow the Platonic idea of the Universal Soul or any other speculation of ancient philosophers, or we might attribute to God a son as Christians do. Thanks to the Qur'an, we Muslims have the soundest beliefs about God.

4. Interpretation of the Divine Acts

It is the Qur'an that best introduces us to God's acts in the universe. Here is an example:

قُلِ اللَّهُمَّ مَالِكَ الْمُلْكِ تُؤْتِي الْمُلْكَ مَنْ تَشَاءُ وَتَنْزِعُ الْمُلْكَ مِمَّنْ تَشَاءُ

وَتُعِزُّ مَنْ تَشَاءُ وَتُذِلُّ مَنْ تَشَاءُ بِيَدِكَ الْخَيْرُ إِنَّكَ عَلَى كُلِّ شَيْءٍ قَدِيرٌ تُولِجُ

اللَّيْلَ فِي النَّهَارِ وَتُولِجُ النَّهَارَ فِي اللَّيْلِ وَتُخْرِجُ الْحَيَّ مِنَ الْمَيِّتِ وَتُخْرِجُ

الْمَيِّتَ مِنَ الْحَيِّ وَتَرْزُقُ مَنْ تَشَاءُ بِغَيْرِ حِسَابٍ

Say: O God, absolute Master of all dominion! You give dominion to whom You will, and take away dominion from whom You will, and You exalt and honor whom You will, and abase whom You will; in Your hand is all good; surely You have full power over everything. You make the night pass into the day, and You make the day pass into the night; You bring forth the living out the dead, and You bring the dead out of the living, and You provide whomever You will without reckoning (Al Imran 3:26–27).

In this way, the Qur'an makes us know of the Divine acts. Without this introduction, we could not know God by His all works.

5. Sacred Map of the Hereafter

The Qur'an is unique in the way it presents to humanity the map of the Hereafter. It shows the stages and places of the afterlife in live scenes so impressive and captivating that are impossible to summarize here.

$$\text{الْحَاقَّةُ مَا الْحَاقَّةُ وَمَا أَدْرَاكَ مَا الْحَاقَّةُ}$$

The Sure Reality! What is the Sure Reality? And what enables you to perceive what the Sure Reality is? (al-Haqqah 69:1–3).

The *surah* of al-Haqqa starts with the reverberation of the fearsome sounds of the great disaster at the end of the day. The *surah* holds our hands and takes us to the moment of that catastrophe. Then it makes the mountains "crushed to powder at one stroke," and making us really look at them. Then it resurrects us to judge our deeds. It puts in Paradise those whose good deeds weigh more, and in Hell those whose bad deeds weigh more. The *surah* illustrates the events of the Hereafter in a vivid tableau that one cannot imagine a more impressive one. It says:

$$\text{يَوْمَئِذٍ تُعْرَضُونَ لَا تَخْفَى مِنْكُمْ خَافِيَةٌ}$$

On that Day, you will be arraigned for judgment, and no secret of yours will remain hidden (al-Haqqah 69:18).

This brings in front of us everything that we try to hide from others, making us feel embarrassed for our improper deeds. The same verse also encourages us to take action not to fall into such a condition. On that day, the poor in terms of good deeds will be given their records from the left hand, while those with abundant goodness from the right hand. The latter will rejoice:

$$\text{فَأَمَّا مَنْ أُوتِيَ كِتَابَهُ بِيَمِينِهِ فَيَقُولُ هَاؤُمُ اقْرَءُوا كِتَابِيَهْ}$$

Then, as for him who is given his Record in his right hand, he will say: Here, take and read my Record! (al-Haqqah 69:19).

The former will remorse:

وَأَمَّا مَنْ أُوتِيَ كِتَابَهُ بِشِمَالِهِ فَيَقُولُ يَالَيْتَنِي لَمْ أُوتَ كِتَابِيَهْ

But as for him whose Record is given in his left hand, he will say: Ah, would that I had never been given my Record! (al-Haqqah 69:25).

6. Book of Law

As a book of law, the Qur'an sets the religious rules, clearly states the permitted and forbidden things, and regulates the life of the individual, family, society, and state. It teaches the principles of a complete system of law.

7. Book of Wisdom

Philosophers typically talk about the ultimate reality of the world. The history of philosophy is full of theories about this inquiry. The way the Qur'an deals with the same great subject is totally different. It is different because the Qur'an is the word of the One who created the world. While philosophy examines the ultimate reality with a hypothetical language, the Qur'an explains it with definite and conclusive statements. While the former is full of controversies and contradictions that confuse us, the Qur'an is far above from any disharmony and confusion.

8. Book of Worship

The Qur'an elevates us to the highest understanding of service to God. A way of worship that is not acknowledged by the Qur'an should be wrong. A yogi stays in a place like a grave for months without eating and drinking. A monk confines himself into the monastery where he endures the hardships of an ascetic life. But these do not have any significance in the sight of God. The Qur'an approaches the human reality in accordance with the integrity of our body and spirit, our mind and heart, and thus requires a way of service to God that complies with this integrity. Our worships will be significant and valuable as long as they comply with the teaching of the Qur'an.

9. Book of Prayer

The Qur'an teaches us how to pray to God the best way. It is so generous in this regard. If we open our hands towards God Almighty with the Qur'anic prayers, we will let the Lord speak on our behalf and ask Him with His own words. This is the Prophet's way, peace be upon him, whose prayers were typically taken from the words of the Qur'an.

10. Holy Book Coming from the Divine Presence

Each Divine Name is reflected the most in certain contexts throughout creation. These special contexts are called by some the "thrones" of the Divine Names related to them, from which God rules those special contexts in the universe. For instance, water can be considered such a throne for the Name of "Muhyi," the One who grants life. Likewise, grains can be said to be a throne for the Name of "Razzaq," the Provider. This figurative language suggests that God's each Name has special spheres of manifestation like a king being called with various titles in different offices in his country. Each event in creation specifically refers to a Divine Name, which lies behind and rules that phenomenon. The universe as a whole is the greatest sphere of Divine manifestation and its immensely vast context is figuratively called al-Arsh al-A'zam, the Greatest Throne. This term is also used to mean the transcendent presence of God, which is infinitely sublime and encompasses the heavens and the earth.

The Qur'an descended from the Greatest Throne, the transcendent presence of God. The Qur'an originated in the highest degree of manifestation of each Divine Name. This is why the Qur'an is the most perfect word of God. It was revealed to the most perfect person and addressed the most perfect community. The title "Word of God" is given to the Qur'an in its fullest sense.

Part Two
Prelude to Al-Fatiha

I.

Isti'adha: Taking Refuge in God from Satan

When we want to recite the word of God, we should prepare our soul for this. This preparation requires freeing and purifying our heart and feelings from the effects of Satan. As God expelled Satan from the heaven eternally, we too must drive him out of our heart, which is essentially more sacred than the Ka'ba and loftier than the highest heaven. We need to do so, that we may acquire God's morals and deserve to get into the Qur'an.

With this consideration, Muslims traditionally start the recitation of the Qur'an, just as many other good deeds, with the saying: أَعُوذُ بِاللهِ مِنَ الشَّيْطَانِ الرَّجِيمِ or "I take refuge in God from the accursed Satan." This practice is established by the Prophet, peace and blessings be upon him, following the Qur'anic order (an-Nahl 16:98). For some scholars like Ahmad ibn Hanbal, Thawri, and Awzai, one should say it as: أَعُوذُ بِاللهِ السَّمِيعِ الْعَلِيمِ مِنَ الشَّيْطَانِ الرَّجِيمِ or "I take refuge in God, the All-Hearing and the All-Knowing, from the accursed Satan."

I. Word Analyses

The phrase "I take refuge"

The Arabic verb أَعُوذُ (I take refuge) is a conjugation from the root عَوْذ which has several meanings. Three of them are: to take refuge, to ask for protection, and to adhere. If we apply these three meanings to *isti'adha*, it will mean:

1. I take refuge in the sanctuary of God's grace and mercy.
2. I ask God for His protection from the Fire, His punishment.
3. I adhere to God's power, relying upon His authority. Despite my personal impotence, I am powerful with His support and can challenge all obstacles. Here I challenge Satan, who sets traps for me.

The word "Allah" or "God"

As the proper Name of the Creator, "Allah" or "God" refers to His transcendent Person that has all Attributes of perfection and is above from all imperfections. God's unique, matchless, transcendent Person cannot be comprehended by human intellect. As His proper Name, "Allah" or "God" denotes all the meanings of Divine Names together. When we say "God" or "Allah," this comprehensive meaning comes to our mind. Likewise, when we say, "I take refuge in God from the accursed Satan," we mean: I take refuge in and rely upon the sublime Creator, who has unique and absolute authority in the universe, from all evils, all evil persons, and all devils that may come to me from any directions or any parts of the universe.

The word "Satan"

There are two possible roots for the word *shaytan* in Arabic.[20] The first is شطن, which means "to be far from something." In this case, the word means: the one who is far from God's mercy.

وَكَذَلِكَ جَعَلْنَا لِكُلِّ نَبِيٍّ عَدُوًّا شَيَاطِينَ الْإِنْسِ وَالْجِنِّ

And thus it is that We have set against every Prophet a hostile opposition from among the satans of humankind and jinn (al-An'am 6:112).

---

[20] The Arabic word *shaytan* is a relative for the English word Satan. The former refers both to any devils and the chief devil named Iblis. Not a proper name but an adjective or noun, *shaytan* can be used in plural form as *shayatin*, namely devils or satans. (Ed.)

As exemplified in this verse, all who have gone (and insist to live) far away from the Divine mercy are called *shaytan* or satan. Likewise, all ways of life that take us far away from God's mercy are the ways of *shaytan*. The second possible root is شاط, which means "to be invalidated." In this case, *shaytan* means the one who invalidates the beneficial things, including his own benefits when he once disobeyed God although obedience was possible.

The word "accursed"

The word الرَّجِيم is an adjective that means "accursed." It particularly refers to Satan as he was cursed by God and expelled from His mercy. We many times are not able to notice the misleading of Satan, or even if we notice, we may not be able to remove it from our heart. It is as if Satan built a station for him in our heart and placed a receiver there for communication. This receiver, a subtle faculty in our soul, is called the "satanic spot" (*al-lumma ash-shaytaniyya*) in Islamic tradition. This is just as we have a faculty in our soul or a spot in our heart that receives God's inspirations. The Qur'an describes Satan as *"sneaking whisperer"* (an-Nas 114:4). For this character, many times we cannot realize what he subtly dictates our heart. In this situation, we appeal to *isti'adha* and say: أَعُوذُ بِاللهِ السَّمِيعِ الْعَلِيم مِنَ الشَّيْطَانِ الرَّجِيم : "I take refuge in God, the All-Hearing and the All-Knowing, from the accursed Satan." In saying "the All-Hearing," we call upon God who hears the hidden voice of Satan in our heart. In saying "the All-Knowing," we call upon God who knows and is capable to remove the effects of this misguidance.

2. The Wisdom behind *Isti'adha*

Our human essence demands isti'adha

As humans we potentially have many enemies and problems. From mosquitoes to malaria, from storms to meteors, many things function against or even threaten our life. We need to overcome all these, either by ourselves or by help of others. On the other hand, we are in need of many things, from the light and heat of the sun to the beauties of Paradise, to the eternal beauty of God. But obviously we are not capable to overcome all our problems and meet all our needs by ourselves. Being aware of this limitation is essential to the true self-knowledge, and this knowledge is the beginning of all true accomplishments.

However, at the first step, the knowledge of our limitations makes us feel weak and impotent or even miserable. We feel disappointed with a serious humility. We feel so deeply hurt that, even if we do not express our need of help, God will definitely have mercy upon us and lend us a hand: This is the second step. The third is "work." We hope God's grace and providence, feel His support with us, and thus seek ways to fulfill our will and intention. At this moment, we express our situation with *isti'adha*. Doing this, we admit that God is the only sanctuary, for He is the All-Powerful and the All-Knowing. There are many who want to be a very good believer with sound faith and practice, but they are often tempted and misguided by Satan. To lead a good life straightforwardly is really hard. Against this hardship, one should take refuge in God and often practice *isti'adha*.

God placed in our nature feelings like desire and anger so that we may be tried with them and thus be trained and develop. The "negative" feelings are our potentials by the means of which we can improve our spiritual capacity. Just as God created the fire for our benefit, He created desire and anger in our nature to the same end. It is thanks to this desire that we have offspring, that humanity gain new generations as servants to God, that the purposes of creation are fulfilled. Although desire is given for such lofty ends, many times it causes us to fall from the heaven of perfection into the darkness of a corporeal life. Similarly, all feelings are given to us for some benefits and yet they may be misused. We often feel exhausted from the struggle to orient our feelings towards their proper ends. *Isti'adha* comes to our help at this moment and supports our morale.

Isti'adha is a sign of fidelity

To say "I take refuge in God" is to express our apology in a sense; it is a sign of our fidelity to God. With *isti'adha* we also admit to God our bewilderment in the face of countless possibilities in course of our life. In the Qur'an, *isti'adha* marks the virtue of loyalty to God in the examples of the Prophets. When Noah, peace be upon him, was reproached

by God upon asking Him to forgive his son who had perished as a disbeliever, Noah appealed to *isti'adha*:

$$\text{قَالَ رَبِّ إِنِّي أَعُوذُ بِكَ أَنْ أَسْأَلَكَ مَا لَيْسَ لِي بِهِ عِلْمٌ وَإِلَّا}$$

$$\text{تَغْفِرْ لِي وَتَرْحَمْنِي أَكُنْ مِنَ الْخَاسِرِينَ}$$

(Noah) said: O my Lord! I seek refuge in You, lest I should ask of You
what I have no knowledge of. And unless You forgive me and have
mercy on me, I will indeed be among the losers (Hud 11:47).

When tempted and intimated by Zuleikha[21], Prophet Joseph, peace
be upon him, too appealed to *isti'adha*:

$$\text{قَالَ مَعَاذَ اللهِ إِنَّهُ رَبِّي أَحْسَنَ مَثْوَايَ إِنَّهُ لَا يُفْلِحُ الظَّالِمُونَ}$$

He said: I take refuge in God! My lord (your husband) has given me
honorable, good lodging. Assuredly, wrongdoers never prosper.
(Yusuf 12:23)

In saying so, Prophet Joseph proved his loyalty to his Lord. A
monument of modesty and chastity, he believed that he could escape
from this difficult situation only by seeking refuge in God, and that was
what happened. Prophet Moses, peace be upon him, is another example. Upon his people's question whether he made fun of them when he
asked them to sacrifice a cow, he replied:

$$\text{أَعُوذُ بِاللهِ أَنْ أَكُونَ مِنَ الْجَاهِلِينَ}$$

I seek refuge in God lest I should be among the ignorant (al-Baqarah 2:67).

From the point of view of faith, anyone who knows God cannot be
called "ignorant" even if he has little knowledge of the world. But anyone who does not know God can be called ignorant even if he has great
knowledge in a science. This verse implies that making fun of some-

---

[21] The wife of Prophet Joseph's lord in Islamic and Jewish traditions. The Qur'an does
not mention her name. (Ed.)

body is something that only the ignorant, those who do not know God, could do.

The Qur'an teaches us prayers of *isti'adha*. To mention a few:

وَقُلْ رَبِّ أَعُوذُ بِكَ مِنْ هَمَزَاتِ الشَّيَاطِينِ وَأَعُوذُ بِكَ رَبِّ أَنْ يَحْضُرُونِ

And say: My Lord! I seek refuge in You from the promptings and provocations of the satans. I seek refuge in You, my Lord, lest they be present with me (al-Mu'minun 23:97–98).

قُلْ أَعُوذُ بِرَبِّ الْفَلَقِ مِنْ شَرِّ مَا خَلَقَ وَمِنْ شَرِّ غَاسِقٍ إِذَا وَقَبَ وَمِنْ

شَرِّ النَّفَّاثَاتِ فِي الْعُقَدِ وَمِنْ شَرِّ حَاسِدٍ إِذَا حَسَدَ

Say: I seek refuge in the Lord of the daybreak from the evil of what He has created, and from the evil of the darkness (of night) when it overspreads, and from the evil of the witches who blow on knots (to cast a spell), and from the evil of the envious one when he envies (al-Falaq 113:1–5).

Isti'adha is to entrust things to God

Mu'adh ibn Jabal, one of the prominent Companions, narrates that two men reviled each other in the presence of the Prophet, peace and blessings be upon him, and one of them became excessively angry so much that his jugular veins swelled. The Prophet, peace and blessings be upon him, said to some other Companions: "I know a phrase which, if he repeated, he could get rid of this angry feeling." They asked: "What is it, Messenger of God?" He replied: "He should say: I seek refuge in God from the accursed Satan." Mu'adh then asked the person to do so, but he refused.[22]

The person disrespected the advice of the Prophet; perhaps he could not get it because of his furious state. The intention of the Prophet, peace and blessings be upon him, was to rescue him immediately from the suffocating atmosphere of his temper. That is to say:

1. The Prophet indirectly advised him: If you say this word, you will leave the matter and Satan to God. Be careful: The acts of

---

[22]　*Sahih al-Bukhari*, Bad' al-Khalq, 11; *Sahih Muslim*, Birr, 109.

revenge that you design in your mind for the man you are angry at will only wear you out and will not do any harm to him. However, if you entrust the matter to God, you will take a best revenge on him.

2. The Prophet implicitly reminded him: Sometimes two persons become rivals and take action against each other without really knowing which side is right or guilty. In such situations, the soundest way is to entrust the matter to God. In saying *isti'adha*, you mean: I take refuge in God from making a wrong decision and doing injustice. Then this word will extinguish the fires set by Satan.

3. The Prophet again implicitly taught him: You dare to attempt to devastate the man with your power. But no matter how powerful you are, God is more powerful. If you do injustice like a tyrant, God may devastate you on the Day of Judgment. Then you'd better take refuge in God, entrusting the case to His justice.

Isti'adha is a shelter against all evils

In a hadith, the Prophet, peace and blessings be upon him, is reported to have said:

> "Whoever dismounts to rest in a place should say, 'I seek refuge with the complete words of God from the evil of what He created,' and nothing will harm him until he remounts."[23]

Everywhere in the universe, the evil ones bother and fight the good ones, be they devils and angels, evil spirits and good spirits, or evil people and good people. The evil ones work to harm humanity, while the good ones work to benefit humanity. For this reason, wherever we go or stay, we should seek refuge in God from all evil ones, even including vermin. This means we ask God's help and the help of all good ones.

Abu Umama al-Bahili, a Companion, was sadly sitting in the mosque. The Prophet, peace and blessings be upon him, approached him and asked what made him so sad. Abu Umama replied: "O Messenger of God,

---

[23] Musim, Dhikr, 54, 55; *Sunan at-Tirmidhi*, Da'awat, 40; *Sunan Ibn Majah*, Tibb, 46.

we as family are suffering poverty; we have nothing to eat at home. So I have come to ask God for help." Then the Prophet, peace and blessings be upon him, taught him the following prayer, each phrase being a gem of a vital truth, to offer in every morning and evening:

> "O God! I take refuge in You from anxiety and grief; I take refuge in You from incapacity and laziness; I take refuge in You from stinginess and cowardice; I take refuge in You from the burden of debt and the domination of people."[24]

The Qur'an, with its hundreds of verses, teaches us, explicitly or implicitly, to take shelter in God from Satan, from our evil desires, and from all evil factors in creation, whether we know those factors or not.

Isti'adha relates to our eternal needs

Our needs extend to eternity. We long for spring or summer, just as we wish to have flowers. But neither of such things can satisfy us. We then wish to attain a paradise, not a temporal, but an eternal one. Even an eternal paradise does not satisfy us, we then wish to see and contemplate God's eternal beauty. In fact, as we are given something, this gives us the idea of asking for more. We are such creatures whose wishes keep coming after one another. But our potentials and abilities are so limited, confined in the circle of the reach of our hand. Even the matters of this small circle overwhelm us many times. What should we do then? The most reasonable thing is to say, "I take refuge in God."

Isti'adha is to admit our weakness

To say "I take refuge" is to admit one's weakness and impotence. With this admission, our heart can better turn to its Lord. Then the Divine mercy will lift its veil and smile at our face, we who are desperately in need of mercy and compassion. Upon this honor of closeness, we will understand the meaning of the Divine saying: "I am with those with broken hearts."[25] If we admit our weakness, saying: "I could not succeed

---

[24] *Sahih al-Bukhari*, Da'awat, 36; *Sunan at-Tirmidhi*, Da'awat, 70; *Sunan Abu Dawud*, Witr, 72.

[25] Sahawi, *al-Maqasid al-hasana*, I, 169; Munawi, *Fayd al-Qadir*, II, 69.

in life, I could not overcome the difficulties of time, I could not manage to do good deeds to win Your pleasure, yet I have now come to Your presence, with my heart broken..." then God will respond to us, saying: "Don't worry, for I am with those with broken hearts."

Isti'adha purifies the heart

To succeed in fully obeying God, we need to drive Satan out of our heart and prepare it for God's presence. When we cannot succeed to purify our inner world and embellish it with virtues, then our recitation of the Qur'an will come out of a stained heart and mouth. Therefore, we first need to purify our heart, and this is exactly what *isti'adha* does. When we say, "I take refuge in God from the accursed Satan," we should consider this purification and believe that this word can do it.

The heart is the house of God, His palace. The Sovereign wants to come into His palace, especially at nights. But such honor requires our preparation of the palace. Concerning this, God's Messenger, peace and blessings be upon him, recommends us to take *wudu*, offer some prayers, and take refuge in God, when we go to bed. For God may come into our heart at night. But this will not happen if our heart is not purified and prepared. Ibrahim Haqqi[26] says:

> The heart is God's house; keep it pure from anything else.
> So the Sovereign would honor His palace at nights.

The Prophet, peace and blessings be upon him, teaches us, using a figurative image, that God comes close to our sky every night and says: "Who is saying a prayer to Me that I may answer it? Who is asking something of Me that I may give it him? Who is asking forgiveness of Me that I may forgive him?" If we prepare our heart for this honor, God will gracefully come into it.

God prepared the Paradise for us, our eternal abode that He calls in the Qur'an as *Dar as-Salam* or the Abode of Peace (al-An'am 6:127; Yunus 10:25). With this title, it is as if God Almighty says to us: "I have prepared the Paradise as a pure abode for those who live in peace and

---

[26] Sufi poet of the late Ottoman times. (Ed.)

purity. I have an abode, too, which is your heart. Do you too keep My abode pure for Me?"

> God said, I am not to be confined in the heavens or the earth;
> But He is known as a treasure in the depths of the heart.

This couplet of Ibrahim Haqqi is an adaptation from the following saying that is narrated as a hadith qudsi[27]:

> "My earth does not encompass Me nor does My heaven, but the heart of My servant, the man of true faith, does encompass Me."[28]

God has chosen our heart for His throne, a special place for His glory and beauty to be reflected. For this reflection to be perfect, we should keep our heart pure and clean.

Isti'adha will provide this purification. This is why the Messenger of God, peace and blessings be upon him, had a habit: When he went to bed, he kept his hands together, recited the last two surahs of the Qur'an, which are two prayers of isti'adha, blew to his hands and ran them on his body.[29] In doing this, he took refuge in God from every evil, aiming to protect his body and soul from the effects of Satan. He warns us, saying:

> "Satan moves inside your veins just as your blood does."[30]

It seems as if Satan rides on the red and white blood cells to enter our heart and inspire us his misguidance. Thus the spiritual atmosphere of the heart gets blurred, while it is the place of Divine manifestation. Then we start to look at our surroundings with blurred eyes and not recognize the fact that everything around us speaks of God. Against this multidirectional threat of Satan, we need to take shelter comprehensively. This is why we say "I take refuge in God," using His Personal Name that is comprehensive to all Divine Attributes. In other

---

[27] A *hadith qudsi* is a Prophetic saying by which the Prophet, peace and blessings be upon him, translates a Divine revelation that is not included in the Qur'an. (Ed.)

[28] Ghazali, *Ihya' 'Ulum ad-Din*, III, 15; Daylami, *Al-Musnad*, III, 174.

[29] *Sahih al-Bukhari*, Fadail al-Qur'an, 15; *Sunan at-Tirmidhi*, Da'awat, 22; *Sunan Abu Dawud*, Adab, 108.

[30] *Sahih al-Bukhari*, I'tikaf, 11–12, Adab, 121; *Sahih Muslim*, Salam, 23.

words, this phrase comprehends all alternative phrases such as: "I take refuge in the All-Merciful One," "I take refuge in the All-Compassionate One," etc.

Isti'adha supports us in our struggle

We may have enemies who threat our personal life, our wealth, our values, or our country. These enemies attack on us with weapons, tanks, and warplanes. When we ask God for help against these kinds of attacks, God will help us with his providence in many ways. Numerous examples can be given from our history. God sent thousands of angels to support the Prophet's army against the attack of Meccan pagans in the Battle of Badr. A similar support is reported to have occurred in the Battle of Gallipoli against the invading forces, even according to General Hamilton's own statement. It is as if the believers asked, *"When comes God's help?"* (al-Baqarah 2:214) and God came to their help.

The struggle against physical enemies is called the "lesser struggle" (*al-jihad al-asghar*) in Islamic tradition. The "greater struggle" (*al-jihad al-akbar*) is against our spiritual enemies, namely Satan and our evil desires, his allies. We should also ask God for help against the attacks of these spiritual enemies. They do not invade our land, but our heart, the palace of God Almighty. Just as God helps us in our lesser struggle, He will support us too in our greater struggle. And the best strategy in this battle is to take refuge in God.

Who is Satan from whom we take refuge?

The Qur'an describes Satan as the "accursed" or "expelled" one (al-Hijr 15:34). From this description, we infer that Satan had once been close to God as an obedient servant. Then he became the victim of his arrogance; he was expelled from God's mercy due to his disobedience and obstinacy. He was driven out from the Paradise prepared for believers. God drove him out so that His good servants would live there in security. Have we succeeded, in return, to drive Satan out from our heart so that God may reside there? This is an important matter that *isti'adha* reminds us each time we repeat it. In fact, a believer is someone who emulates the Divine morals. As God dismissed Satan from our eternal place of peace, we should dismiss him from the precious place of Divine manifestations in us.

The definite article in the word الشَّيْطَان (literally, the satan) indicates that the devil in question is the one who rebelled against God in the beginning for the enmity to Adam and humanity. It is this Satan that institutionalized unbelief, establishing a legacy of disobedience. Just as he has done in the past, he will always work in this cause, trying to destroy or at least disturb the Divine order, until the Day of Judgment. He will always find representatives for his mission. The definite article also implies: "Satan is your old enemy since the time of your first ancestors. He will try to do to you whatever he did to Adam and Eve. So do not make him your friend. Be alert against his enmity and take refuge in God." On the other hand, if the definite article modifies a kind or species, then the word denotes all members of the "accursed" from the time of Adam to the present.

II.
Basmala: "In the Name of God"

"**B**asmala" is the collective name in Arabic for the phrase بِسْمِ اللهِ الرَّحْمَنِ الرَّحِيمِ which is often translated as "In the Name of God, the All-Merciful, the All-Compassionate." *Basmala* is the beginning of all good works. It is like a luminous rope dropped down to humanity from the Divine presence. A man who holds tight this Divine rope can challenge the entire universe. The universe was founded and the life on earth started "in the Name of God." All events in nature take place "in the Name of God." The Last Day will be realized, all people will be raised from the dead "in the Name of God." The gate of Paradise will be opened when the believers say, "In the Name of God," and they will witness there the All-Merciful and the All-Compassionate. This temporal world will come to an end with *basmala*, as it started with it.

I. The Preposition " ـبـ "

The preposition (ـبـ) at the beginning of *basmala* means "with" in Arabic, and thus the literal translation of the phrase is: "With the Name of God." Grammatically, the preposition (ـبـ) is connected to a verb, which is not uttered. For instance, if we say *basmala* at the beginning of the act of eating, we mean: I am beginning to eat in (or "with") the Name of God. As "with" signifies togetherness and closeness, it can be said that whoever wants to be "with" God should often practice *basmala*. The preposition also denotes adherence. When we say *basmala*, we adhere to God's mercy and compassion.

The preposition (ب) allows an implicit commentary in Sufi understanding. Sufis say that all the mystery of existence reveals itself in the ب of *basmala*. If we remove the dot under the letter, it becomes a line, like the line that comprises the first Arabic letter: *alif* (ا). This line is infinite and—just *alif* symbolizes God in Sufi tradition—implicitly refers to God, particularly His infinite preexistence to the creation. Until the creation came into reality, God had not been known by anybody else than Himself. This is like the letter ب being unidentified unless we put a dot under the line. The following Divine saying famous in Sufi tradition illustrates this truth:

> "I was a hidden treasure and I wanted to be known. So I created the creation so that I may be known."[31]

In Sufi tradition, the dot under the line of the letter ب symbolizes the entire creation before the transcendent and infinite existence of God. All humanity is included in this tiny dot. When the great Sufi ash-Shibli was asked who he was, he replied: "I am the dot under the luminous straight line, as a shade to make its light known." On the other hand, the dot particularly symbolizes the existence of Prophet Muhammad, peace be upon him. God's infinite and unknown existence became revealed at the first time with the Prophet whose spiritual truth preexists the creation of the universe. This "Muhammadan truth" is like the seed of the creation. The Prophet, peace and blessings be upon him, is reported to have said: "*The first thing God created is my light.*"[32] If God had not created this light, God would not be known. God knows Himself eternally, but He wanted to be known by others. To this end, God created the light of the Prophet first, and out of this light, He created the universe, and finally He created the human being like a fruit of the tree of creation. This is what we understand from the Sufi saying: "God is seen always in the mirror of Muhammad."

What appears in this Muhammadan mirror is summarized in *basmala*. First of all, the focus of *basmala* is God's mercy and compassion,

---

[31] Sahawi, *Al-Maqasid al-Hasana*, I, 521.
[32] Suyuti, *Al-Hawi*, I, 325.

which is also the most prevailing character of the Prophet, peace be upon him. God describes His Messenger in the Qur'an as "kind and merciful" (at-Tawbah 9:128). Likewise, God emphasizes the same character of the Prophet in the verse:

وَمَا أَرْسَلْنَاكَ إِلَّا رَحْمَةً لِلْعَالَمِينَ

We have not sent you (O Muhammad) but as an unequalled mercy for all the worlds (al-Anbiya 21:107).

2. The Word "name"

We say, "In the Name of God," instead of saying, "In God." This shows the significance of "name" in *basmala*. First, if we were to say the latter phrase, which literally is "with God" or "by God," that would mean swear in Arabic. But we do not mean to swear to God. We mean to act by asking God for His providence and blessing and by committing ourselves to His will. Ultimately we mean to be elevated to the heights of the spiritual reality from the pits of a corporeal life. We say *basmala* in order ultimately to ascend the sky of human perfection.

The word "name" evokes God's all Names, which are described in the Qur'an as the "Most Beautiful Names" (*al-Asma al-Husna*) (al-A'raf 7:180). God's Names are mostly associated with His acts. For instance, we call Him "ar-Rahman" (the All-Merciful One) for His acts of mercy. In truth, God can be called with as many Names as His acts in the universe. As mentioned above, the name "God" or "Allah" implicitly denotes all Divine Attributes. Thus, when we say "In the Name of God," we actually mean, and tacitly mention, all Divine Names. In other words, with *basmala*, we appeal to God not only with His Names "the All-Merciful" and "the All-Compassionate," but also, in our intention, with His other Names: the Provider, the Creator, and so on. We appeal to these Names as our intercessors in the presence of God.

We say *basmala* in a position where we call upon God from distance, where we call upon Him with the pronoun "He." This position is called *ghaybuba* (absence, distance) or *farq* (difference, separation) in Sufism. This Sufi understanding seems to be supported by the fact that, in *basmala*, we do not appeal directly to God's Person, but to His name.

The Name of God denotes our infinite distance or difference from the transcendent Divine Person. Besides, the word "name" evokes the manifestations of God's Names throughout the universe, which again evokes "distance" or "transcendence" between our persons and His.

3. The Word "God"

The existence of everything depends on God. The light on the face of the universe is the word "Allah" or "God." When this word is missing, all sciences and all knowledge are doubts and delusions, a heap of inexplicable ideas. The deadlocks and congestions in contemporary sciences originate in this missing. Today all sciences and technologies not based on the word "God" are facing doubts and hesitations at their foundations. Today scientists attempt to "explain" the reality of phenomena by theories and hypotheses, which are not capable to reveal their ultimate meaning.

Everything in existence depends on a truth. This magnificent universe must depend on a great truth, which would give the universe its ultimate meaning. The existence of the human being, this monumental creature, cannot depend on amoebae or worms, or the winds of coincidences. There must be a great truth as a basis of this monument. This truth is the word: "God, the All-Merciful, the All-Compassionate." The fundamental problems that face today's sciences and philosophies can be cured by this key word. This is a task that the sincere believers should undertake.

If all sciences should be re-organized, this should be done on the basis of the word "God." Only then can sciences and scientific education be based on a truth and find their meaning. It is the believers that will give science its new course. Knowledge will be based on sound foundations by their hands. Otherwise, the universe will be destined to nonsense and wasted in vain. A meaningless universe is not the purpose of the Creator. This is why God will destroy the universal order at the end of the time.

God is veiled from our sight. We cannot see Him with our eyes. He is transcendent. We do not see Him but we see His works manifest in everything. We understand that God is hidden due to the intensity of His manifestation. God is the only One who is worthy of worship. He is the only true Beloved. So our hearts can find satisfaction only when we remember God. All broken hearts attain peace and integrity when they reach God. He is the unique shelter for all those with a broken heart. God is exalted and far above from the considerations of the unbelievers. He is the source of awe and admiration for the believers. Everyone who increases his knowledge about God will be deeply amazed and filled with awe.

The words associated with the Name "Allah"

Although scholars suggest some etymological analyses for the origin of the word "Allah" in Arabic, my heart does not tend to reduce the Name of God to some ancient human words. I rather feel that, as the Creator is eternal, so is His Name. He is eternally "Allah." However, it is a linguistic fact that there are some words in Arabic which look to be associated with this Divine Name. Below are the suggestions of Arabic linguists.

Alaha (اَلَه)

The generic noun الِٰه (*ilah:* "god" or "deity") comes from the verb اَلَه (*alaha*). This verb means to find peace and satisfaction in somebody. We humans tirelessly work for peace and satisfaction. This persistent orientation and activity are required by our own human essence, namely our heart and conscience. We will move from our basic humanity upward, traveling with awe to the realm of the Divine Names and Attributes, and finally the transcendent Divine Person. In return to this consistent effort, God will grant us the perfect peace and satisfaction that we long for. God is the final destination of those who seek peace and satisfaction.

$$أَلَا بِذِكْرِ اللهِ تَطْمَئِنُّ الْقُلُوبُ$$

Be aware that it is in the remembrance of God that hearts find rest and contentment (ar-Ra'd 13:28).

Aleha (اَلَه)

This verb is a version of the above one and has several meanings. One is to take shelter in somebody, like an infant taking refuge in her mother. For their weakness, babies take refuge in the compassionate bosom of their mothers. So are the servants of God: Out of weakness and impotence, we take refuge in God's mercy. God is the only true sanctuary. Another meaning of the verb is to serve or worship. In relation to this root, "Allah" means the worshipped one. God is the only one that deserves worship. A third meaning of the verb is to protect something or somebody. This relates to God's protection over His servants.

Walaha (وَلَهَ)

Another possible root verb is وَلَهَ , which means to rise or be elevated. God is transcendent, far above from time and space. He governs the universe and rules over everything. He is exalted from all kinds of improper imaginations of the unbelievers. He is exalted from their arrogance when they say, "We observe the universe, but we don't see God anywhere." The meaning of "loftiness" or "transcendence" is associated with the word "Allah" and inferred from behind it.

Besides, *walh* (وَلْه), a noun derived from the same verb, means awe or amazement. We feel awe in the face of the Divine glory, a deep feeling that is somehow shared by all humanity. In this sense, the awe of God is a manifestation of the light of the Divine unity. Some people experience it in a basic level, although some others lose the sense of personal identity in the face of the glorious Divine manifestations.

Laha (لاَهَ)

This verb means to be hidden. God cannot be seen with eyes although He is absolutely manifest in the universe. He is out of our sight due to the perfection of His existence, due to the intensity of the light of His manifestation. What we see in this world are all imperfect existents, which have their kinds and opposites. God is the One whose transcendent existence is the unique source of all phenomena. How can we claim to see Him? For ages, the people of the heart, the heroes of spirituality have been offering their prayers, calling: "O my God, He who is hidden for the intensity of His manifestation! O my God, He who is unseen for the perfection of His light!"

To summarize all these meanings: God is the sanctuary of the weak and poor. He is the Lord that is served and worshipped. He is the remedy of our afflictions, the cure of our wounds and sufferings. He is the light of the universe. All matters can be resolved with Him. When we find Him, we are liberated from destructions that the overwhelming events otherwise might cause.

An outstanding feature of the word "Allah"

The word الله (Allah) in Arabic has a special feature that no other words display. If we remove the first letter *alif* (ا), there remains another word: لله (*lillah*), which means "for God." If we remove the next letter *lam* (ل), there remains another word: له (*lahu*), which means "for Him." If we remove the next (again ل), there remains a pronoun: ه (*hu*), which means "He" or "Him." This latter has a special significance in Sufi tradition: It is expressed in remembrance of God (*dhikr*) in the place of God's Name. In this case, it is written as هو and pronounced with a long u.

Among Sufis, هو is considered one of the greatest Names of God. Many times it is better to call upon God with this pronoun instead of His other Names, for it is abstract and directly refers to the Divine Person. When we recite "هو" this makes us contemplate the following way—or the following contemplation makes us recite it: "What am I, compared to You! I am a tiny creature made out of a drop of base fluid, whereas You are the Lord, the King of eternity. I prefer calling upon You with هو , which denotes all Your Names at once. I can extinguish the fire of my heart only by reciting this Name of Yours."

When we recite a Divine Name, we often consider its relations to creation and particularly to us. For example, when we say, "Ya Karim!" ("O the Most Generous!") we consider God's bounties and blessings upon us. When we say, "Ya Jamil!" ("O the Most Beautiful!) we consider God's beautiful manifestations in nature and our life. Although this consideration is good, it may bother a bit the sense of "purely turning to God." However, when we say, "هو" we purely turn to God's transcendent Person, without any other considerations or expectations. This practice satisfies our heart in such a way that cannot be articulated. It has a special impact on our soul and thus plays a special role in spiritual training.

God introduces Himself to us with His works and acts. We can know Him to the degree of our awareness of these Divine manifestations in and around us. Therefore, our knowledge of God is always relative and short compared to an ideal or possible one. Obviously, our personal consideration cannot cover all Divine manifestations throughout the universe. To overcome this relativity or shortage, we recite "هُو" for it purely refers to God's transcendent Person as He is. In the presence of God, we often feel our humility so much that we cannot call upon Him directly and say, "You." As we have said above, هُو is very helpful in this humble situation. Again, in God's presence, when we purely turn to Him, we forget everything, even our own existence. Only His person remains in our consciousness. It is again هُو that can best express our feelings at that moment. In fact, we practice this in every breath: This single syllable is expressed, even unwittingly, with every breathing in and out. In a sense, هُو is the source of our life; we cannot live without it.

4. The Names "ar-Rahman" and "ar-Rahim"

Rahman is both an adjective and noun in Arabic. Literally, it means "the most merciful." As it is particularly attributed to God in Islam, it is used as a Name of God. When we say "Rahman," we only mean God. This is abundantly exemplified in the Qur'an. To mention a few:

$$\text{الرَّحْمَنُ عَلَى الْعَرْشِ اسْتَوَى}$$

The All-Merciful has established Himself on the Throne (Ta-Ha 20:5).

$$\text{الرَّحْمَنُ عَلَّمَ الْقُرْءَانَ خَلَقَ الْإِنْسَانَ عَلَّمَهُ الْبَيَانَ}$$

The All-Merciful has taught the Qur'an, created man, and taught him speech (ar-Rahman 55:1–4).

Rahman is an Attribute particular to God. People cannot be named or called *Rahman*. Due to this particularity, it is not fully proper to translate the Divine Name *Rahman*, just as the Name "Allah." Both are used as a proper name, and we know that proper names are not to be translated. As for *Rahim*, it is an adjective and noun, too. It is also a Divine Attribute, but it is not particular to God. People can be named "Rahim" in the literal sense of the word, namely "compassionate."

Both *Rahman* and *Rahim* are derived from the root *rahma*, meaning "mercy" or "compassion." Then both Names denote God's mercy and compassion. But traditionally, *Rahman* is interpreted as denoting God's all-encompassing mercy over the universe, while *Rahim* denoting His compassion over each and every creature. In other words, *Rahman* more relates to the general manifestation of God's mercy, whereas *Rahim* to the particular. The first case is called *wahidiyyah*, while the latter *ahad-iyyah*, in Sufi terminology, and both terms denotes the "oneness" or "unity" of God.

Rahman relates to eternity, while *Rahim* to perpetuity. For the infinite mercy expressed in *Rahman*, God created the universe out of nothing. Trees, birds, people, all nature come into existence for the manifestation of this Name. All creatures necessarily obey God's commands under the rule of this universal mercy. In this sense, *Rahman* denotes necessity. When God creates, He does not ask anything or anybody whether they want to be created. This necessity or compulsion is a consequence of the *wahidi* manifestation of Divine mercy. He is *Malik al-mulk*, the Owner of all sovereignty. He rules His kingdom howsoever He wills. Nobody can interfere with His rule.

If we considered the reality only from the point of view of *Rahman*, then all opposites and contrasts would look mixed and relative: faith and unbelief, justice and injustice, right and wrong, beautiful and ugly, good and evil. For the free will does not matter in the necessary processes in creation. This would be a morally-neutral universe, in which people would be no different than other kinds of creatures. If the universe had been dominated only by the manifestation of *Rahman*, there would not be a world of moral test and responsibility. But God willed otherwise and granted us free will. That is, God manifested Himself also with His name *Rahim*, which allows personal accountability and hence reward and punishment. In this way, humanity is granted the chance to rise to the highest of the high—of course, at the expense of the risk to fall to the lowest of the low.

If a bird flaps her wings around her babies, if a tree grows and bears fruit, if waters flow and cascade, and if an animal mother treats her young with compassion, all these occurs thanks to the Name *Rahman*. But these creatures do not have free will; they live according to the necessary rules that God determined for them and taught them. However, the particular manifestation of Divine mercy relates to free will, and this is signified by the Name *Rahim*. That is to say, if *Rahman* had not existed, we would not have come into existence. If *Rahim* had not existed, we would not have had free will or understood the subtleties of the Divine creation.

Rahman unfolded the universe before us like a great book, whereas *Rahim* gave us the will to read this book and benefit from its lights in the form of faith and wisdom. *Rahim* enabled us to discover the mysteries of the universe, approach the realm of the Divine Names and Attributes, and contemplate the transcendent Person of the Creator. However, it is not possible for us to comprehend His transcendent Person. All the Names and Attributes we learn from the revelation are only helpful to some extent; they cannot fully reveal the transcendent Essence of God. Concerning this, Abu Bakr, may God be pleased with him, is reported to have said: "*The true comprehension is to understand our incapacity of comprehension.*"[33] Likewise, the Prophet, peace and blessings be upon him, is reported to have said: "*O the Known! We could not know You as You truly are.*"[34] We too admit our incapacity and proclaim, in the words of Ziya Pasha:

> This tiny intellect is not to comprehend the lofty truths.
> For this scale cannot weigh this much weight.

5. Some Qualities of *Basmala*

Given the considerations above, we can say that an adequate translation of *basmala* is not possible. In every attempt of translation, some aspects of the original meaning will be lost. This original meaning is so rich that it summarizes all the truths that the Qur'an teaches us. *Basmala* is extraordinary in this respect, and this quality permeates its

---

[33] Ghazali, *Ihya 'Ulum ad-Din*, IV, 252; Suyuti, *Sharh Sunan Ibn Majah*, I, 103.
[34] Munawi, *Fayd al-Qadir*, II, 410; Alusi, *Ruh al-Ma'ani*, IV, 79.

effects in our life. Concerning this, the Prophet, peace and blessings be upon him, says:

> "Any significant work that is not started with 'In the Name of God, the All-Merciful, the All-Compassionate' is fruitless."[35]

The Qur'an teaches four fundamental tenets: *tawhid* or the Divine unity, *nubuwwa* or Prophethood, *hashr* or resurrection, and *adl* or justice. All these tenets are summarized in *basmala*. First, the word "Allah" explicitly denotes the Divine unity. The Name *Rahman* implicitly denotes the Divine act of sending Messengers. The Name *Rahim* again implicitly indicates the comprehensive principle of justice in life and the resurrection of the dead for the final judgment.

Basmala takes place in the beginning of each *surah* of the Qur'an except for the ninth one. It is a religious rule to recite *basmala* at the beginning of any Qur'anic recitation, as we do before reciting Fatiha in *Salah*. It is also a religious rule to recite *basmala* before slaughtering animals.

Some scholars consider that each *basmala* at the beginning of the Qur'anic *surahs* is a Qur'anic verse, namely part of the Divine revelation. Others do not consider it part of the revelation, but part of the *surah*. Either part of the revelation or not, it opens each *surah*, separates them from one another, and helps us understand the message of every *surah*. *Basmala* is like a key for each *surah*, just as it is a key for everything in life. It is a luminous line extending from the Divine presence to our hearts. Those who truly understand its lofty meaning and benefit from its blessing can ascend the heaven of human perfection.

God explained the truths of creation in the Books that He revealed. The same truths were finally explained in detail in the Qur'an, the last and universal revelation. Fatiha summarizes the Qur'an and is summarized in *basmala*. That is to say, *basmala* is a link connecting all Prophets and Divine Books to one another. *Basmala* contains the seeds of all truths of creation. But not everyone can manage to discover them.

---

[35] Ghazali, *Ihya 'Ulum ad-Din*, I, 206; cf. Ahmad ibn Hanbal, *Al-Musnad*, II, 359; Daraqutni, *Sunan*, I, 229.

III.
Harmonious Relation between
Basmala and Fatiha

P arts of the Qur'an are harmoniously related to one another. The *surahs* and verses are so coherent that it is as if the Qur'an was revealed at once to address to a single event. We observe the same coherence between *basmala* and Fatiha. But before explaining this, it would be good to mention a couple of linguistic matters.

A word can denote a meaning in three ways:

1. The literal or apparent meaning, which is what we commonly and easily understand from a word. It is the meaning for which the word is put forth first of all. For example, when we say "اَلْحَمْدُ لله رَبِّ الْعَالَمِينَ" its apparent meaning is: "All praise is for God, the Lord of the worlds." This is what we understand from the word immediately.

2. The literary or rhetorical meaning, which we may not understand easily. This understanding requires a careful approach to the word. Regarding the same example, if we ask why "praise" is attributed to God instead of "thanks," the answer would reveal a literary meaning that is not apparent in the sentence.

3. The intuitive meaning, which comes to our mind or heart in a subtle way. This kind of hidden meaning is available to those with spiritual maturity and sensitivity. It can also be called inspirational meaning.

It is an overwhelming task to study the Qur'an at these three levels. Our subject is Fatiha and I will only attempt to point out some aspects of the rich content of this great *surah*. My purpose is to provide a humble example in this regard.

I would like to mention another issue by the way. Although studying the Qur'an is a necessary task, *Salah* (Daily Prayers) is not a good venue for this. It is not considered good to reflect elaborately upon the verses we recite while praying, for this would bother our feelings in Divine presence. We rather should ponder upon our stance in His presence, upon the Divine grace and majesty manifest in the essence of the revelation. This spiritual concentration would help us feel awe more deeply and be more respectful to the Lord.

* * *

Fatiha has various names, as mentioned before. For instance, it is called *"as-sab' al-mathani"* (al-Hijr 15:87) which roughly means "the repeated seven," referring to the number of its verses. The Prophet, peace and blessings be upon him, also called it *"umm al-kitab"* (the mother of the book), *"ash-shafiya"* (the healer), and *"al-wafiya"* (the complete and perfect). Fatiha is a Divine treasure. Everyone facing a problem can find its solution in it. It is a mysterious *surah* that brings people closer to God, their Lord.

There is a strong relation between Fatiha and the *basmala* that precedes it, just as between Fatiha and the *surahs* that come after it. These relations constitute part of the context of a *surah*. Each word should be taken in its context and Fatiha allows such contextual treatment.

As Fatiha is a prayer taught by God, then we can assume the *surah* to be preceded by a silent Divine command such as "Recite!" or "Say!" A historical narrative about the beginning of the Qur'anic revelation supports this point:

In the days before the first revelation, God's Messenger, peace and blessings be upon him, had a habit to retreat to a cave on the Mount Hira. He was full of concerns about the severe condition of his community and humanity's salvation in general. He sometimes heard a voice on the mountain and in the wilderness, calling him, "O Muhammad!"

Since he was worried about the matter, he returned to home when it happened. His dear wife Khadija advised him to consult her cousin, Waraqa ibn Nawfal, who was a Christian convert and knowledgeable about the nature of Divine revelation. He also expected the advent of a new Prophet whose signs he had seen in the Gospel. God's Messenger, peace and blessings be upon him, told him about his experience and the voice calling him. Waraqa advised him not to worry but stay and listen to what it says. The Prophet, peace and blessings be upon him, did the same. Then the angel Gabriel, the owner of the voice, started to reveal the Divine words. According to this narrative, Fatiha was the first revelation and it started with Gabriel's word: "Recite in the Name of God: All praise is for God, the Lord of the worlds..."[36]

Basmala is connected so strongly with Fatiha that it is like a part of it. In fact, many scholars consider *basmala* to be the first verse of the *surah*. There is a poetic relation between them. *Basmala* is not only a prelude to Fatiha, but also a prelude to creation. As passed above, *basmala* tells about God's unique eternity, His eternal mercy and generosity, and the "Muhammadan truth" that was the luminous seed out of which all creation came into reality. After this prelude, Fatiha starts with praise to God.

* * *

God's mercy is a powerful source of attraction in *basmala*. This attraction has an impact on everything connected with *basmala*, and Fatiha is not an exempt. When we recite *basmala* before Fatiha, this practice evokes the questions: "How should I respond to God who introduces Himself as the All-Merciful and the All-Compassionate?" Our answer to this question is what we recite right after *basmala*, the very first sentence of Fatiha: "All praise is for God, the Lord of the worlds." We mean to respond to the infinite mercy that encompasses us, with unlimited praise and gratitude. In other words, with the meaning revealed between *basmala* and Fatiha, God teaches us how to respond to the endless manifestation of His mercy. He teaches us how to respond to being created from nothing first of all, then to being granted faith, being Muslims,

---

[36] Ibn Abi Shayba, *Al-Musannaf*, VII, 329; Bayhaqi, *Dalail an-Nubuwwa*, II, 158.

and being followers of the Messenger of mercy. In another perspective, all these merciful bestowals make us say, "All praise is for God, the Lord of the worlds." By saying this, we mean: All praise and thanks be to God, who brought us into reality, made us human, made us believers, and made us followers of a religion that is the greatest humanity.

In reciting *basmala*, in proclaiming the unity of God and His infinite mercy, we are reminded of the manifestations of these Divine truths in all creation. We are reminded that God has prepared the earth for us as a grand feast, that the entire universe is an immense ocean waving with mercy. In response to these reminders, we say, both on our own behalf and on behalf of other creatures: "All praise is for God, the Lord of the worlds."

* * *

When we say, "In the Name of God," we do not call upon Him directly. In *basmala*, we do not say, "In Your Name." In this regard, *basmala* implies our distance and difference from God. To enter the special Divine presence, we need to travel spiritually. We need to contemplate the Divine manifestations and understand His glory and beauty, and then we can turn to Him and call upon Him directly. Before such a spiritual ascent in our inner world, we feel our distance and difference by default. This is why the starting point of our prayer, which is *basmala*, is not a direct address to God.

However, as we contemplate the creation "in the Name of God," we feel that we get closer to God. Contemplation brings us to the level of consciousness that we perceive God beyond all phenomena. We perceive God's act of beautification in the face of a flower, His act of organization on the body of a tree, and so on. These perceptions warm our heart and lead us to the special Divine presence. Then we feel we are in a close position where we can call upon Him with "You." In other words, we feel we are in a context that is a mixture of the Divine Names: *Awwal* (First), *Akhir* (Last), *Zahir* (Apparent), and *Batin* (Hidden). The same context is where we start to call upon God directly in Fatiha, saying: "*You alone do we worship, and from You alone do we seek help*" (al-Fatiha 1:5).

We proclaim our service to God at this very moment of meeting with Him. For one should present a gift to the king upon entering his presence. Our best gift to present to our Lord is obviously our service to Him: our sincere recognition of His unique authority and our deep respect to His will. Only with this presentation of service can we enter the special Divine presence and call upon Him directly. The need of direct address to God is intrinsic to our soul. But we need first to purify our feelings and thoughts to be prepared for directly speaking to Him. Upon this preparation, we can aptly say: "*You alone do we worship.*"

Worshipping God alone in a consistent way is an overwhelming task and it requires asking God for help. This is why we add: "*And from You alone do we seek help.*" In the position of closeness we have attained, we can seek help only from God. For we have contemplated His glorious power over everything. Having arrived at His special presence, we feel that we have an opportunity which we must benefit from in best way; we must ask God for something that is worth most. This is why we ask for guidance, the most important matter for us: "*Guide us to the straight path*" (al-Fatiha 1:6).

When we start Fatiha, "the Lord of the worlds" introduces us to the truths of all creation. Namely, in this phrase, we contemplate the true relationship between the universe and its Master. We understand the true nature of phenomena through this concept of the universal Lordship. All laws of nature operate according to this Divine title. But most of natural phenomena look unfriendly or even scary. If we consider the universe only with reference to "the Lord of the words," then we only feel awe. But at this point, the Names *Rahman* and *Rahim* come to our help and make us feel comfortable. Since the Lord of the worlds is the All-Merciful and the All-Compassionate, there is no need to be scared in the universe. Moreover, He is "*the Master of the Day of Judgment*" (al-Fatiha 1:4). We are comforted ultimately with the fact that there is a day on which the righteous will be generously rewarded and the unrighteous will be justly punished. We find a sufficient reason for being peaceful in this Divine Attribute. It articulates that God is powerful enough to resurrect the dead on a coming day for a final judgment.

To conclude, we understand that *basmala* is strongly related to Fatiha and the latter has a harmonious flow from the beginning to the end. Fatiha compared to the rest of the Qur'an is like a star in the sky, which is both independent from and connected to the other celestial bodies. Fatiha is a single *surah*, yet it is connected to all parts of the Qur'an. In fact, the Qur'anic verses are also called "*najm*," which literally means shining star. Just as the stars, parts of the Qur'an display a great order.

Part Three
Commentary on the Verses

I.
"All praise is for God, the Lord of the worlds."

I. The Word "Praise"

Fatiha starts with the word *hamd*, which is often translated as "praise." But the meaning of *hamd* is more comprehensive than praise. *Hamd* is basically a respectful and thankful response to God who owns the universe, bestows upon us life and provides us with all the blessings as a manifestation of His infinite mercy and generosity. But *hamd* does not only mean to thank God for His kindness. We also express with it our unconditional praise and gratitude that God absolutely deserves. In other words, to say our *hamd*, it is not necessary that we have been granted a particular blessing as it is the case with *shukr* or "thanking." *Hamd* is first demanded by the very character of the Praised One, who is necessarily worthy of worship. This is why Fatiha starts with "All praise is for God," instead of "Thanks be to God."

We thank God for specific blessings, and we can express this gratitude with our words and acts, or even silently in our heart. All prayers, particularly *Salah*, are a form of gratitude, an embodied sentence: "Thanks be to God." Similarly, the feeling of gratitude itself is a silent word and it says the same sentence.

Hamd is also different from *madh* or "compliment." It is possible to laud the living and nonliving alike, which is not the case with *hamd*.

We praise God as He is eternally alive and infinitely glorious and beautiful. Although we can praise people just as we should thank them, our praise for them should be moderate and should remind of God's grace. We should put a balance in this matter and not neglect what people really deserve. The Prophet, peace and blessings be upon him, says: "He who does not thank people does not thank God."[37]

Gratitude is the mark of the faithful people. The number of truly grateful people seems to be few. God's blessings are numerous, endless. In his *Gulistan*, Sa'di Shirazi says that one owes two thanks to God for each breath. God grants us our life twice in each time we breathe in and out. We should respond to this consistent bounty with gratitude and let it be expressed with our tongue, acts, and heart. Gratitude is a serious responsibility; there are a few who fulfill it truly. The Qur'an says: "*Few are the truly thankful among My servants*" (Saba 34:13). Faithfulness requires thankfulness.

Hamd is superior to gratitude in that the former signifies our unconditional service to God, regardless of whether we have received a specific blessing. It is the expression of the voluntary, sincere turning to God. We say it without any expectations. Thus it is the mark of sincerity. *Hamd* is the point where we recognize and understand the unconditional, immutable Divine goodness. Let me give an example: If we receive a gift from a king, we know that there are two aspects of its value. First, its material value that is limited to its physical size and quality. This size and quality, in turn, limit our material pleasure out of the gift. The second aspect relates to the source of the gift, the fact that it is directly from the king. The physical size and quality are irrelevant to this aspect. Our spiritual pleasure and joy out of this fact is much more than the former. Our soul reaches the king's will or even himself through the gift, which is most important. Likewise, it is much more important to attain God through *hamd* than to simply benefit from His blessing.

Man is both the praising and praised one. We praise God and are praised on the earth and in the sky. In fact, "Muhammad" and "Ahmad," the two names of the Pride of Humanity, are derived from this truth.

---

[37] *Sunan at-Tirmidhi*, Birr, 35; *Sunan Abu Dawud*, Adab, 11.

These names are all about *hamd*, the very linguistic root of them. As the Prophet, peace and blessings be upon him, served God in his life, God praised Him and made this manifest in the Prophet's name, which utterly means "the praised one." As for "Ahmad," it also means "the praising one." That is to say, the Prophet, peace and blessings be upon him, combined the virtue of praising God and being praised by Him. This privilege is called *al-maqam al-mahmud* (the praised position) in the Qur'an (al-Isra 17:79). It is a Muslim tradition to offer a prayer after *adhan* and ask God to raise the Prophet, peace and blessings be upon him, to the utmost degree of this *al-maqam al-mahmud*. In the Hereafter, the Prophet, peace and blessings be upon him, will hold the "standard of praise" (*liwa al-hamd*) as mentioned in a hadith. People will be secured under this banner, and when they enter the paradise, they will say: "All praise be to God." Concerning this, God's Messenger, peace and blessings be upon him, says: "My people are called *hammadun*, the praising ones."[38]

It is reported that the caliph Umar asked Ali ibn Abi Talib: "After each daily prayer, we recite *Subhanallah* (Glory be to God), *al-Hamdu lillah* (All praise is for God), *Allahu akbar* (God is the greatest), and *La ilaha illallah* (There is no god but God). We comprehend all these but *al-Hamdu lillah*. What does that word really mean?" Ali, may God be pleased with him, replied: "It is a word which God appropriates for Himself and with which He is pleased."[39] This answer reveals a subtle point about the truth of *hamd*.

The Prophet, peace and blessings be upon him, tells that a servant of God once offered a prayer: "O Lord! Praise be to You as much as befits Your glory and majesty!" This was too much for the two angels to record. They did not know how to record it. So they soared to the heaven and said: "Our Lord! Your servant said something which we don't know how to record." God asked them although He surely knew what the servant had said: "What did My servant say?" They replied: "He said: O Lord! Praise be to You as much as befits Your glory and

---

[38] Suyuti, *Ad-Durr al-Manthur*, VI, 332.
[39] Ibn Abi Hatim, *At-Tafsir*, I, 27.

majesty!" God said to them: "Write it down as My servant said it, so that he should meet Me and I reward him for it."[40]

In another hadith, God's Messenger, peace and blessings be upon him, says: "To say 'All praise is for God' will fill the scale in the Hereafter."[41] In fact, to praise God sincerely will fill the scale of goodness in the Hereafter.

2. The Word "Lord"

In Arabic, *rabb* is a noun and means "lord" or, more precisely, "one who provides and cherishes." The phrase "the Lord of the worlds" does not only denote God's ownership over the whole creation, but also His all-encompassing providence over the universe. Consider the Divine providence over the realm of humanity: God guides us in life, invites us to the eternal rewards of Paradise and warns us against the punishment of Hell. He sent to us the last Messenger, peace and blessings be upon him, and encouraged us to follow him. God revealed the hidden truths in the Qur'an and thus enlightened our soul. All these signify His lordship which the word *rabb* perfectly means. In fact, this word denotes all Divine acts at once.

It is God that cherishes and sustains all creatures. God provides for all creatures according to their particular natures He sets for them. We observe that all creatures obey the Divine providence. God is the One who provides for humanity, too. And the most important aspect of this special providence is that He sent Messengers to help us distinguish the right path from the wrong. Humanity can reach maturity and perfection only by obeying the Divine laws, and the soundest way of this obedience is to follow the Qur'an. As opposed to naturalistic philosophy, the Qur'an teaches us that the principle of life in nature is cooperation, not enmity. If the soil embraces the plant like a compassionate mother, how can we call this a struggle? In fact, the laws of nature are the ways of this cooperation. Inanimate matters help the plants

---

[40]   *Sunan Ibn Majah*, Adab, 55.

[41]   *Sahih Muslim*, Tahara, 1; *Sunan at-Tirmidhi*, Da'awat, 85; *Sunan an-Nasa'i*, Zakah, 1. Here "scale" figuratively refers to the Divine means to measure the good and bad deeds on the Day of Judgment. (Ed.)

live, the plants help the animals live, and all help humanity live in this world. This chain of cooperation means the pathway of perfection for the entire nature.

God operates the universe through the laws He set, and guides all creatures towards maturity and perfection through them. God does so for the purpose of distinguishing the good from evil, the luminous from the dark, and the diamond from the coal. Through this process, the righteous get prepared to enter Paradise while the unrighteous prove to deserve a punishment. As God distinguishes these groups in this world, He will do the same in the Hereafter. The only prevailing reality in the universe is God's providence, the clear manifestation of His all-encompassing lordship. If we can truly contemplate the realm of humanity, this can suffice to prove this truth and we will not need any further proof.

God has absolute authority over the events. He initiates and maintains the natural phenomena for certain purposes, and in this way, creatures are directed towards maturity and perfection. Take as an example the creation of an infant: The real "reason" behind its formation is not the sperm or egg. The true reason is the Divine will which causes the formation of the infant in the womb in an ultimate way. The principle of causality is meaningful only when we consider the Divine will behind the process. This is like we cannot attribute the formation of a magnificent palace to a child deprived of the knowledge of engineering. Physical forces in nature are not functional by themselves, but they are utilized and governed in the course of natural processes. God is the ultimate power behind the great event of creation. Indeed, it is impossible to understand how the disbelievers can insist on the rejection of the idea of the Divine creation. All phenomena embellished with proofs from the earth to the sky indicate God's existence and unity. Disbelief is not only a strange attitude, but also a terrible ingratitude and rebellion.

If the natural phenomena are studied from the point of view of faith, then science will become the source of true wisdom, and nature will turn into a book. If we look at ourselves from the same perspective as the Creator look at us, namely if we examine ourselves according to the Qur'anic guidelines, we will be in a condition much different than the one we are facing today.

God created humanity out of His mercy and generosity, and He sent the Qur'an to help us find our way as a result of the same Divine Attributes. The Qur'an is an ocean of Divine mercy, and it addresses the mankind whom God created "in the image of *Rahman*," as mentioned in a hadith.[42] If we truly understand the responsibility that this privilege requires, then we will understand the meaning of the Prophetic saying: "If you knew what I know, you would laugh little and weep much."[43] Or even we will say, like the Prophet: "I wish I was a piece of wood instead of a man."[44] Indeed, a look to ourselves from the heaven of the Divine Attributes will make us feel the deep responsibility of being human. This is possible only if we can delve deep into the ocean of the Qur'an or soar throughout its starry sky.

In the Era of Happiness, namely the time of the Prophet, peace and blessings be upon him, people looked at themselves in this way, and they found themselves. Then God gave them authority over the world. This was a manifestation of the fact that God made humanity His "vicegerent" on earth. When we turn to God fully with our mind and heart, He will manifest the truth of His saying:

$$\text{وَلَقَدْ كَتَبْنَا فِي الزَّبُورِ مِنْ بَعْدِ الذِّكْرِ أَنَّ الْأَرْضَ يَرِثُهَا عِبَادِيَ الصَّالِحُونَ}$$

We wrote down in the Psalms after the Torah that My righteous servants will inherit the earth (al-Anbiya 21:105).

Indeed, God has always entrusted His inheritance to His righteous servants. For this reason, the only authority was Muslims on the land in the Era of Happiness.

God has established a strong relationship between Himself, the universe, and humanity. He has placed man before Him and addressed him with a "you," and allowed us to address Him directly. God has placed the sphere of "service" against the sphere of "Lordship." He has shared

---

[42] Tabarani, *Al-Mu'jam al-Kabir*, XII, 430.
[43] *Sahih al-Bukhari*, Kusuf, 2; *Sahih Muslim*, Kusuf, 1.
[44] *Sunan at-Tirmidhi*, Zuhd, 9; *Sunan Ibn Majah*, Zuhd, 19.

with us the meaning of His Names *Rahman* and *Rahim*, which He has taught us in *basmala*. And finally we are taught to say, "All praise is for God," in response to all these.

3. "All praise is for God" and the Principles of Faith

The word *al-Hamdu lillah* (All praise is for God) indicates, explicitly or implicitly, all principles of Islamic faith. Let us now talk about this.

Belief in God

We praise God for His works and prostrate ourselves before His glory with awe and admiration. We are enraptured with love in the face of His beauty. We thank Him with humility in the face of His blessing. And *hamd* signifies all these. As mentioned above, the Name "Allah" etymologically means the One who is worshipped, obeyed, taken refuge in, relied upon, and admired with awe. Therefore, when we say "al-Hamdu lillah," we praise God whom we uniquely worship and absolutely trust, and whom we ask for our needs. We also mean to deny divinity to anyone else. In a sense, *al-Hamdu lillah* is an expression of *La ilaha illallah*: "There is no god but God."

All truths of creation spring from the single word: "There is no god but God." With this sacred word, the believer is distinguished from the disbeliever, and the sincere devoted from the hypocrite. "There is no god but God" is like a mark or sign by which a part of humanity is distinguished from another part. But to utter this word cannot make us attain the mentioned privilege. Instead, it should be the expression of our deep-rooted faith. Indeed, our faith is revealed when this sacred word manifests itself as a deep understanding, when it governs our feelings. Otherwise, no sacred words can truly signifies faith, just as we cannot get warm only by saying "Furnace!" or "Fire!" or as we cannot be cured from a poison only by saying, "I will be fine!" If ours is to be called true faith, we should believe that God is the only One worthy of worship at least as much as we believe that fire is burning and poison is fatal. Ideally, one should see Him as the only wisdom behind all phenomena, the only Reason to understand anything. Only then will our word

"There is no god but God" be in harmony with what we hold in our heart. Only then will be truly believers.

As believers, we are convinced that all natures in the universe are bound to the will of God. Fire does not necessarily burn or poison does not necessarily kill by their natures: They affect by God's will. The nature of anything is created by God. This is the creed of *Ahl as-Sunnah*, the mainstream Muslim theological school. As fire is effective only by God's will, it did not burn the Prophet Abraham, peace be upon him (al-Anbiya 21:69). Likewise, as God willed it, a poisoned food did not kill our Prophet, peace and blessings be upon him, although the same food killed the Companion who took a bit from it.[45] Such extraordinary incidents show that it is only God that brings the events into existence. A believer should think about nature in this way. This metaphysical perception will bind our soul to the heaven while we are bound to the earth with our body. This faith will make us feel attached to the temple; we will feel regretful when we are deprived of service to God.

We always feel a hidden power that attracts us towards the high horizons of existence where we find true peace. We submit our will and intellect to this power that attracts us towards eternity. This submission will lead us to Paradise and God's eternal beauty, which can uniquely satisfy our soul. Faith will bring to us *yaqin*, the utmost confidence about what we believe. This *yaqin* will turn our heart into a mirror in which the eternal beauties are reflected. Finally, our homes and society will radiate the lights and scents of the Divine realm.

Service to God is inherent to our nature. God created humanity with a temperament that tends to be a servant to God. But throughout history, we have many times abused this nature, when people worshiped objects like the sun, stars, stones, or other creatures of God, which are never worthy of worship. Whenever people replace the only God with the things He created, they fall from the high honor of service to God to the disgrace of paganism. Yet even pagan culture indicates the inherent sense of service to God in our nature. When people are misguided

---

[45]   *Sunan Abu Dawud*, Diyat, 6.

and lost their true God, this nature is degenerated and directed to the invented, false deities.

Islam is the religion of *fitra*, the pure Divine creation. This religion is also called *hanifiyya*, meaning to worship solely God. The Prophet Abraham, a great leader of this path, shows us the way to ascend towards God by denying authority to any other things. As narrated in the Qur'an, he refused the sun, moon, and stars to be deities as they set and disappear (al-An'am 6:76–79). When we truly understand this Abrahamic message, we will say like him:

$$\text{إِنِّي وَجَّهْتُ وَجْهِيَ لِلَّذِي فَطَرَ السَّمَوَاتِ وَالْأَرْضَ}$$

$$\text{حَنِيفًا وَمَا أَنَا مِنَ الْمُشْرِكِينَ}$$

I have turned my face with pure faith and submission to the One Who has originated the heavens and the earth each with particular features, and I am not one of those associating partners with God. (al-An'am 6:79).

The deep sense of Divine unity will bring us up to the heights of the service to God, where we will understand what humanity truly means. And we will attain this deep sense when we truly follow God's Messengers. In their luminous path, the curtains will be lifted from the eyes of our hearts and we will face with God. This final attainment is all about the practice of pure service to God. Books cannot explain it. Even the eminent friends of God are unable to articulate it. Except for a few privileged ones, most of people cannot feel it even when reciting the Qur'an. This is a direct experience that does not allow any intermediation. In this spiritual rapture, we lose our own self, feeling only awe and admiration. What can one say in this situation? In history, some Sufis said: "There is no existent but He." Some others said: "There is nothing observed but He." And some others chose to say: "I do not see around but His manifestations." Howsoever one expresses his spiritual experience in this position, it will not mean but a little approach to what really happens. Words are not helpful to reveal its truth at all.

Our faith in God, our deep experience of Divine unity brings "peace" to us. In fact, consciously saying "All praise is for God" is an instance of such inner peace. Unity is necessary and essential to divinity. It is impossible to consider God without His unity. There is no room in the universe for any associate or partner for God. As traditionally argued, multiple gods would interrupt each other's work and this would lead the universe to a total chaos. A real authority does not accept any interruption or intervention. There cannot be multiple chief administrators in a town or a state. The precise order in nature shows that the Creator has no partner in His authority. In respect to His power, there is no difference between the creation of an atom and that of the universe. God creates a human person and the whole nature with the same power. For Him, bringing the Paradise into existence is no more difficult than a flower. Therefore, the assumption or imagination of a partner in divinity is not but a mental disorder that would disrupt our peace of mind and heart and destroy the unity of our thought.

لَوْ كَانَ فِيهِمَا ءَالِهَةٌ إِلَّا اللهُ لَفَسَدَتَا فَسُبْحَانَ اللهِ رَبِّ الْعَرْشِ عَمَّا يَصِفُونَ

Had there been in the heavens and the earth any deities other than God, both (of those realms) would certainly have fallen into ruin. All-Glorified God is, the Lord of the Supreme Throne, in that He is absolutely above all that they attribute to Him (al-Anbiya 21:22).

Adhered to Divine unity, we do not venerate the natural causes as naturalists do. We do not let our love of anybody to confuse the sense of worship in our heart. We do not love even the Prophet, peace and blessings be upon him, in a way that may bother the sense of Divine unity in our soul; we avoid the mistake that Christians make. Rather, we observe a balance: We recognize divinity only to God and accept the Prophet as our guide and intermediary towards Him. For the Prophet, peace and blessings be upon him, received the last commands from our unique Lord, he saw all metaphysical realities that we believe, he saw even God, and he called us to faith with an utmost confidence. His pure and sincere proclamations have been truly echoed in the hearts of his believers for ages. Imagine that the waves he caused in the ocean of wisdom are still reaching at the shore of the twenty-first century. His first proclamation, "There is no god but God," this purest expression of Divine unity, indicates that the Prophet Muhammad, peace and blessings be upon him, is the greatest to invite to the One God.

A believer who attributes everything in the universe to God's power will establish a relationship with all creatures. There will be no loneliness, animosity, or fear in his soul anymore. He will become friend to the earth, birds, trees, all animals and plants. The believer looks to the universe as a cradle of friendship. For everything comes from the "One" and will return to the "One" in the end. Until our bodies will be resurrected, our soul will remain bound to God. Then we will see our Lord in Paradise and witness His infinite existence directly.

The Messenger of God, peace and blessings be upon him, was exhausted when he was on the way back to Medina from the Battle of Uhud. His head was wounded and his teeth were broken. He had lost a victory because some of his companions did not fully obey his command.[46] Nonetheless, the Prophet, peace and blessings be upon him, did not feel bad towards the place of the battle. Instead, expressing his sympathy and friendship for all creation, he said: "Uhud is a mountain that loves us and we love him."[47] This sympathetic word caused peace and confidence in the souls of the companions so much that perhaps they could not feel better with another word. From another perspective, the Prophet, peace and blessings be upon him, seemed to comfort the Mount Uhud since it was frightened as many believers were killed and God's Messenger was injured around it.

On another occasion, Uhud quaked when the Prophet, peace and blessings be upon him, was on it together with his friends. He ordered: "Uhud, stop! For a Prophet, a truthful one, and two martyrs are standing on you." Upon this command, the mountain stopped to quake.[48]

---

[46] In the battle, the Prophet, peace and blessings be upon him, deployed a group of soldiers on a hill to defend the passage between two mountains and commanded them to stay there even if they had seen him killed on the battleground. However, this group left the hill to join the army when they assumed the fight was over, which gave the enemy a second chance to attack on Muslims from their behind. (Ed.)

[47] *Sahih al-Bukhari*, Zakah, 54, Jihad, 71.

[48] *Sahih al-Bukhari*, Fadail al-Ashab, 5, 6; *Sunan at-Tirmidhi*, Manaqib, 18. In this word, "the faithful one" refers to Abu Bakr, and "two martyrs" are Umar ibn al-Khattab

This was a miracle, and it too shows that God's Messenger, peace and blessings be upon him, had strong relationship with all creation, that he saw the universe as a cradle of friendship. It is well-known historically that he had dialogue with creatures: stones, animals, and trees. There is a serious lesson in this attitude of him that we should take. And such a lesson can be completed only by deep faith in Divine unity, the sacred principle that connects everything to each other.

Summarizing all these, God's Messenger, peace and blessings be upon him, says: "The best word that I and all Prophets before me have ever said is: There is no god but God."

Belief in God's Angels

The word "All praise is for God" implies the belief in God's angels. For this word tells that God deserves praise in a loftiest manner. However, men are not perfect and thus unable to practice this purest duty. This shows that there must be the kind of servants who do not know disobedience to God or neglect to serve and praise Him. There are such noble servants of God and they are called *malak* (angel) in the language of Islam.

"All praise is for God" also encourages us to emulate the angels in their service to God. Those who want to serve God without disobedience and neglect should take the example of angels as much as possible. On the other hand, when we emulate the angels in our devotion to God, we can become superior to them due to the value of our struggle against the short aspects of our nature. Ibrahim Haqqi tells this truth as follows:

> Angels are God's noble servants in the heavens and on the earth.
> But God made humanity superior to them potentially.

Unlike us, the spiritual ranks of the angels are fixed. They were created as to obey God absolutely and they fulfill their duties as God commands them. The Qur'an says:

and Uthman ibn Affan, who would be killed after the Prophet in their respective times of caliphate. (Ed.)

لَا يَعْصُونَ اللهَ مَا أَمَرَهُمْ وَيَفْعَلُونَ مَا يُؤْمَرُونَ

They do not disobey God in whatever He commands them, and carry out what they are commanded (at-Tahrim 66:6).

Humanity was created as God's vicegerent on earth. In order to fulfill our duty of gratitude in response to this privilege, we should live, like angels, according to the purpose of our creation. We should obey God at least in the way that the rest of the universe show respect to His will. Both the heavens and the earth "willingly" obey God's command (Fussilat 41:11).

Belief in God's Books and Messengers

"All praise is for God" also implies that God revealed His will and wisdom through the mission of His Messengers. Praise be to God who sent the Qur'an to us. We have learned from the Qur'an how to serve and praise God, and how to respect God's messages and Messengers. We could not know these without the Qur'an been revealed. We serve God according to the program that the Qur'an shows us. It is this sacred program that makes our worship distinct from those presented to idols or totems.

"All praise is for God" is all about service to God and this service is possible only by the mission of God's Messengers. For otherwise we cannot know how to serve Him. God wants us to know and serve Him through the contemplation of this universe, His work. Then a teacher is necessary, whom God would train and appoint to explain the true meaning of the universe and the true service to Him. "All praise is for God" expresses our gratitude to God for sending Prophets to guide us. And this expression is connected to the name of the last Prophet, "Muhammad," which utterly comes from the word *hamd* or praise.

Belief in the Hereafter

The sincere practice of *al-Hamdu lillah* reminds us of the resurrection after death. If a blessing is not persistent in any way, it cannot be called a blessing at all; rather, it is a punishment. And punishment will turn one's love into hatred and enmity. The countless blessings prove that

God Almighty wants us to know, love, praise, and thank Him. He will never let this praise and gratitude come to an end. For this reason, He will never cease the manifestation of His mercy and generosity. He will always let us praise and thank Him in an everlasting life. We live with His praise, will be revived with His praise, and when we enter the Paradise, we will say:

الْحَمْدُ لله الَّذِي صَدَقَنَا وَعْدَهُ وَأَوْرَثَنَا الْأَرْضَ نَتَبَوَّأُ مِنَ الْجَنَّةِ حَيْثُ نَشَاءُ

All praise is for God, Who has fulfilled His promise to us, and has made us inheritors of this land, so that We may dwell in Paradise as we please! (az-Zumar 39:74).

4. The Word "the worlds"

The original word is الْعَالَمِينَ and it means "the worlds" or "the realms." The definite article "al-" proves that the word refers to all worlds God created. The singular form of the word (*alam*) comes from a root that means "sign." This etymology is traditionally associated with the truth that all realms in creation—from the atomic world to galaxies—are signs that indicate the glory of the Creator.

The universe is such a unique, beautiful work of art that we observe the Divine truth in it. We witness in every aspect of this creation the beauty and glory of the Creator. But this requires the ability to see and discern subtleties, a gift that is given to those who consistently reflect and contemplate. Nothing in the universe has been created in vain, and this wisdom can be attained by a consistent contemplation. This wisdom opens for us new horizons to understand our Creator, the Lords of the worlds.

In the time of the second caliph Umar, may God be pleased with him, grasshoppers suddenly disappeared around Medina as if they were extinct. The caliph was so sad about it. He asked people traveling through the country to let him know if they see any grasshoppers. One day, a man coming from Yemen brought him a handful of grasshoppers. Upon this, Umar said: "God is great." Then he explained this: "I heard the Prophet, peace be upon him, saying: 'God created thousands of nations in animals, some in the oceans and some on the earth. The first among them to be extinct is grasshoppers, then others will follow them one by one.' So I got worried that the order of the world would deteriorate during my rule and this would mean the coming of the end of the time."[49] In this word of Umar, we can discern the wisdom mentioned above.

A contemporary scientist once said about the threat of extinction of the bald ibises: "All creatures are the complimentary parts of the universal order God established. When one of them is lost, this great order loses one of its components. Even the smallest or disgusting creatures have significance in this great harmony. God completed His wisdom with each of them. A loss among them will cause subsequent losses just as a problem in our body causes successive complications."

* * *

As the Lord of the worlds, God provides for all creatures in all realms in the universe. Nothing can be mature and perfect without His providence: The seed cannot become a plant, a tree cannot bear fruits, the sugar cannot be separated from the cane, and the air cannot be purified without God's grace. God creates living creatures out of lifeless materials like stones. He brings the dead to life and turns the simplest things into the most perfect and lofty beings. God's providence in creation inspires us awe and makes us prostrate ourselves before Him.

God's providence aims to carry the creatures to the furthest point of maturity they can reach. If a plant has a nature to bloom, this is the furthest point for it to reach. If a tree has a nature to bear fruits, this is its furthest point. If such a tree has not borne fruit yet, that means it has not reached perfection yet. This is true for the animals, too. Even the snake has a point of maturity in its nature. God's providence leads all elements of nature to their respective perfect forms. It seems as if all nature experiences ascension.

Humanity has its own furthest point of perfection and this is represented in the heavenly ascension of the most perfect man, Prophet Muhammad, peace be upon him. He reached that highest position by

---

[49] Bayhaqi, *Shu'ab al-Iman*, VII, 234; Khatib al-Baghdadi, *Tarikh Baghdad*, XI, 217.

Divine grace and providence. In his ascension, he exceeded the boundaries of this realm of multiplicity, truly understood the Divine unity, and returned to be with us to passionately guide us to this unity.

As Divine providence leads everything to perfection, all members of nature signify the Divine unity. At times, we come across ordinary scenes of creation, like a scrubland or a jungle, and the apparent disorder makes us oversee the Divine providence behind the scene. In reality, there is profound orderliness at every level of nature, so we necessarily attribute all objects and events to God's will and power. The universe appears to us as refined, improved and completed by its Lord. Every creature celebrates the praises of God and we almost hear their voices. Listening to this celebration, we understand the meaning of the "Lord of the worlds."

The furthest point of perfection that we can reach is shown to us by the heavenly experience of our Prophet, peace and blessings be upon him, and this ascension ended up with his meeting with God in a transcendent manner. He attained a position in between eternity and contingence, namely he gained the ability to observe both the Divine and natural realms at the same time. The way to this lofty attainment is open to all. Each of us should seek this path to rise towards the point of perfection that is reserved for us. We should check our current position and ask whether we have fulfilled our task to ascend our own heaven of perfection.

God guides everything in the universe to certain ends. His providence encompasses the whole nature, every single creature in it. Thanks to this grace, molecules are formed out of atoms, and cells are formed out of molecules. Then cells are utilized for the formation of systems in the body. Likewise, countless systems are created out of different materials on the earth and in the heavens. All these are the "worlds" that the "Lord" governs.

* * *

God is the lord, cherisher, and sustainer of all worlds. Grammatically, الْعَالَمِينَ is a plural form that is exclusively used for people or conscious beings. This is a reference to the significance of the human existence in the midst of all realms in the universe. It is humanity that can uniquely understand God's work in creation. The universe would be meaningless without this understanding. With our consciousness, we have brought to the universe value and meaning. Angels and jinns are conscious, too. But they are unable to understand many things as much as the human beings can understand. The grammar inspires another idea: It seems as if the unconscious part of the universe has been melted into the conscious one so that the former too should understand the wisdom of creation.

The universe celebrates the praises of God like a glorious garden signifying the abilities of its owner or designer. If it was written "There is no god but God" with the stars in the sky, this would not be more expressive to proclaim the Creator than the current miraculously shining face of the heaven. From a flower on the earth to the depths of the sky, everything in the universe is taken care of continuously that this magnificent order keeps going on. This continuous phenomenon proclaims "There is no god but God" with an eternal language. That is to say, all creatures in the universe act as if they all are conscious to recognize God; they deserve to be considered among the conscious realms that the word العَالَمِينَ refers to.

* * *

All human individuals need spiritual and moral training in order to be beneficial to themselves and society. Otherwise, they are subject to decay. Just like trees, we are expected to bear fruits, and this goal is to attain human maturity and perfection. Without education and training, we are destined to being spoiled just as milk will be spoilt if not processed. There is a correlation between the nature of humanity and that of milk. In his heavenly journey, the Prophet, peace and blessings be upon him, was presented with a cup of milk and a cup of wine. He looked at them and took the milk. Gabriel, his companion during the journey, said: "Praise be to God who guided you to the true human nature. If you took the wine, your followers would go astray."[50]

---

[50] *Sahih al-Bukhari*, Anbiya, 24, 47; *Sahih Muslim*, Iman, 246, 259.

Like milk, if humanity is left unattended, it will get spoilt. It will not be useful anymore. But if it is processed, it will be useful in many ways. The human individual is the same: If he is not taken care of, if not educated in moral and spiritual ideals, he will be useless. Our education should follow the Divine guidance, the providence that governs the universe. We should join the fortunate ones who walk on God's path. Otherwise, we cannot preserve the purity and value of our own creation. We will attain the high moral ideals if we observe the imperatives that God's Names articulate. This is the only way for us not to fall and become miserable.

Wrong interventions will corrupt the human nature. The true training should follow God's instructions since God is the Maker of the universe and humanity. Imagine a beautiful poem of twenty couplets. We add two couplets in it without reading and studying it, and then we ask anyone who is not knowledgeable about poetry to speak about the poem. Undoubtedly, he will say that the two additional couplets are not suitable to the rest of the poem. Likewise, the universe is a great poem and its all parts are related to each other harmoniously. Humanity has been designed as the greatest couplet of this universal poem. Generations should be raised in accordance with the truths of the universal creation, the truths that we learn from the Divine revelation. We are unable to fully know our true nature by ourselves. We are not capable to reveal the subtle aspects of our spiritual existence by the means of human discovery. Our own judgments about our own existence are not more reliable than those about the universe.

* * *

For a long time, we have followed our own ideas about how to raise the new generations. We have written psychological and pedagogical books on the subject. In this modern period, psychologists and pedagogues have put forth big words. But the attraction of these words originated in their incomprehensibility. Yet they have influenced many and convinced them that these new methods are the true ways to educate the youth. Here are the generations that we have educated with those methods! The youth are now hostile to their own educators, parents, ancestors, and history; they are rude to the social order, sacred values, and the whole nature. Today's world testifies to the fact that the only true training for humanity is the one that follows the Divine guidance.

Wrong interventions have made the new generations deviated. The youth have been offered poison in the place of the water of life. Suppressive coteries, incompetent in knowledge and thought, have played games on the young generations and used them for their own ambitions. These false social engineers used them for their experiments, which resulted in many diseases. They defined humanity according to the negative aspects of their own personality. As a result, many nations and governments have collapsed, and nobody felt remorse for them. Until the day we return to our true essence and recognize our relationship with God, this deviation will go on. Such a return and recognition is possible only through the guidance of the Qur'an and the Prophet, peace be upon him.

We can reach the horizon of human perfection only by going through the "straight path," which in turn goes through the Divine morality. No human philosophies—no matter how masterfully they might be presented under scientific names—can be a good alternative to this path. Instead, they will deal blow to humanity under the name of "treatment." An education is assessed by its results. Here are the streets! The savage of the ancient times could not commit in their lifetime the murders that are done in a few minutes today. In the past, the wildest murderer could kill several people in their entire career. But today thousands of people are killed by the weapons of mass destruction. And the saddest of all is that humanity watches these atrocities and destructions silently and apathetically.

Today's education is unable to stimulate and cultivate the humane aspects of our souls. In this context, lots of scientific theories do not help but make us more doubtful about ourselves. Technology does not help but increase our power of destruction, making us more monstrous than the barbarians of the former times. As the generations have not been guided to the moral and spiritual ideals, rather to the material ones, today the evil aspects of humanity have haunted in a way that it is so hard to discipline it once again.

The young generations in the West have been degenerated and the same is threatening the Islamic community. Muslims too have been spoiled by the philosophy of individualism, and many of them now do not recognize the traditional values. Our society has been suffering from the emergence of such new people. They have authority over the society although they do not deserve it at all, and thus they mislead our people.

Our political life is totally heartrending. Following the pragmatic thinking, political life has venerated "benefit" and "utility" so much that it has finally become the slave of personal interests. In this corrupt context, even a devil would be accepted as if he is an angel just because he may share the same political opinion. Or, an angel would be rejected as if he is a devil just because he may hold an oppositional political opinion. This wrong view is an outcome of the false education given to our generations.

God gave humanity the loftiest honor when He made us His "vice-gerents" on the earth. This means that we should represent God by holding a spiritual mirror to Him and indicate God with our willpower in the universe. But this enormous capacity brings the risk of corruption, a failure that the angels were concerned about when they asked God: *"Will You create someone who will make mischief and shed blood?"* (al-Baqarah 2:30). It seems as if the angels saw the destructive and anarchist aspects of our nature.

* * *

God is the Lord of the worlds, Whose Names are manifested in the universe. According to these manifestations, everything in nature proceeds towards perfection: rocks crumble to be soil; soil opens its bosom to vegetation; plants sacrifice themselves to feed animals and thus rise to the level of animal life; and animals give themselves away to humanity as they desire to rise to the level of human life. In this way, creatures run towards perfection, but at this final point starts decay.

God wants us to participate in the universal move towards perfection. We cannot stay motionless while the entire universe moves. We cannot remain fruitless while everything in nature bears fruits. The best fruit we can bear is the knowledge and service of God. If we fail to love God for our desire of a temporal life, this means our life is pointless and corrupt. For humanity has been designed as a mirror to reflect the Divine Names. God wants us to manifest willingly these Names, being "merciful," "generous," "conscious," etc. We are expected to utilize all these potentials in a right and straight way. God placed rich ores in us. If they are processed through Divine guidelines, they will become infinitely precious. If they are left unattended or processed through non-Divine guidelines, they will be corroded and demolished.

* * *

We should work to fully reflect the meaning of the Divine Name *Rabb* (lord, cherisher, provider). We should be so close to God in respect to this Name that our life may be a perfect example of moral and spiritual maturity. The Prophet, peace and blessings be upon him, reminded people around him of God in a wordless manner when they saw him praying and acting in society. He was described as "someone in whose manners God is manifest." Those who saw him gained confidence about God. If the youth are educated towards this Prophetic ideal, they can be perfect examples of moral and spiritual maturity and they can have a great impact around them. Family and society can find their maturity through this way.

It is naive to expect the generations to be saved from moral and spiritual decay unless we truly educate them. The essence of this education should be to work enthusiastically to help the youth turn to God. If we wish a social order that complies with the teaching and practice of God's Messenger, peace and blessings be upon him, we have to work to this end, and, most importantly, we have to turn to God as he did. He trained his community in moral and spiritual values so perfectly that they became fully prepared for great tasks. On the day of the Battle of Badr, the Prophet, peace and blessings be upon him, raised his hands and asked God for victory. He said: "O God, if we get defeated here, there will be no one left on earth to remember your name." He was so sincere and insistent in his prayer that he did not notice that his robe dropped from his back.[51] Responding to his prayers, God sent

---

[51] *Sahih al-Bukhari*, Maghazi, 4; *Sahih Muslim*, Jihad, 58.

angels to help the believers against their enemy. The Prophet, peace and blessings be upon him, always did his best and then trust in God for the consequences. When we sincerely turn to God, He will help us and we will win a victory against our evil-commanding desires. God will directly guide us and bestow upon us good manners as He has done to many generations before.

The manners that oppose to the Divine guidelines are misbehaviors. Any moral understanding that does not lead to spiritual perfection and the final point of "becoming" is flawed. Morality must be complete. If it does not help us attain the loftiest ideal of humanity, it should be false. This loftiest ideal is the attainment of spiritual perfection here in this world and the Hereafter. And this is possible when we renounce our selfish desires and are annihilated in God's will.

II.
"The All-Merciful,
the All-Compassionate."

I. The Emphasis on Divine Mercy

The two Divine Names *Rahman* and *Rahim* are repeated in Fatiha after they are mentioned in *basmala*. Actually this is not a repetition within Fatiha if we consider that *basmala* is not part of the *surah*. In case of *basmala*, God introduces Himself with His greatest Name "Allah" and then shows that the greatest aspect of His divinity is mercy and compassion. In a sense, God comforts us with this stressed reference to mercy, after mentioning His Personal Name that first reminds of His infinite glory. He enables us to understand His glory along with His mercy.

From another perspective, the Names *Rahman* and *Rahim* encourage us to deepen our relationship with God. Namely, after the Name "Allah" has inspired us awe and fear at the first time, the Names "the All-Merciful" and "the All-Compassionate" make us feel easy. This is a style of the Qur'an: Whenever it gives a warning, an encouragement follows it, or vice versa. And it is also a Divine habit best explained in the following verse:

نَبِّئْ عِبَادِي أَنِّي أَنَا الْغَفُورُ الرَّحِيمُ وَأَنَّ عَذَابِي هُوَ الْعَذَابُ الْأَلِيمُ

Inform My servants that I surely am the All-Forgiving, the All-Compassionate, and that My punishment is indeed the painful punishment (al-Hijr 15:49–50).

In a hadith, God's Messenger, peace and blessings be upon him, says:

"If the believers knew God's punishment, none of them would have any hope of attaining His paradise. If the unbelievers knew God's mercy, none of them would despair of reaching His paradise."[52]

Fatiha displays a similar pattern: When we recite, "All praise is for God, the Lord of the worlds," this inspires us awe and fear, but right after that, we recite, "the All-Merciful, the All-Compassionate," which make us feel peaceful. In these Names, we find God's special treatment with. It seems that these Names tell us: "Do not fear so much, for mercy is the foundation of God's creation. He created you for His mercy, and prepared everything you need for His mercy. As this temporal life cannot satisfy you, He prepared for you an eternal paradise where you will contemplate directly His infinite beauty. He will honor you with this eternal blessing, again, for His mercy."

How nice is that we feel comforted after feeling fearful! How sacred and blessed these two Names are! And how beautiful it is that they follow the phrase: "God, the Lord of the worlds."

2. Transcendent Essence of Divine Mercy

We well know mercy and compassion as a spiritual experience in our heart. Both denote a sympathetic feeling that causes us to act kindly. Some theologians comment that this feeling does not befit God in its human sense; therefore, the fact that God has mercy upon us means that God grants us blessings. But if we take this interpretation, we should apply it to all other Divine Attributes for the same reason, and this would lead us to negate the real meaning of all Divine Attributes.

Another interpretation is possible. It is to affirm for God the real meaning of His Attributes without considering them "identical" to the corresponding qualities we have. For example, God really "sees" and "hears" but He does not need any means for this. We see and hear by means of light, air, and sense organs, so we can see and hear only a limited range of reality. Obviously, this human way of perception cannot be attributed to God. However, we can still believe that God really sees

---

[52] *Sunan at-Tirmidhi*, Da'awat, 99; Ahmad ibn Hanbal, *Al-Musnad*, II, 334.

and hears in a transcendent way. Likewise, we can perfectly hold that God's mercy and compassion are real. He really has mercy upon us in a transcendent way. His mercy and compassion are different than ours just as His seeing and hearing are. With this moderate interpretation, we do not need to deny the real meaning of the Divine Attributes by assuming them to be figurative.

3. Manifestations of Divine Mercy

God creates everything out of nothing. He brings us into existence to manifest His eternal mercy and generosity, and then He sustains our life by providing our needs. He gives us free will to show us the depth of His mercy and generosity, and He will reward us according to the quality of our use of this willpower and freedom. He warns us not to step out of the sphere of His good pleasure, which may cause punishment in the Hereafter.

Imagine a magnificent palace that is furnished and decorated wonderfully. We are invited to this palace along with many other people as guests for a feast. We see there an usher, a representative of the owner of the palace to guide the guests throughout their visit. We see some special marks like medals on his garment that indicate his special position in the palace. We see that he is respected everywhere and obeyed by everybody in the palace. Then we understand that this official is very close to the owner of the palace. Likewise, the universe is a palace built by God and humanity is the noblest part of it as God's representative. We are close to God the most. We are not like animals or plants. We have been given privilege and superiority over the rest of the creation, an honor that demands our responsibility.

Now, would it be appropriate for us to busy ourselves with things that are not pertinent to our privileged personality and special responsibility? How could we direct our attention to some insignificant things like tiny insects or garbage we come across somewhere in the palace? How could we forget that we wear a special garment and represent the owner of the palace? How could we neglect the fact that such irresponsible attitude would cause our punishment? Indeed, we are expected to be aware of our special position near God and act accordingly.

Fatiha gives the guidelines of our proper relationship with God. A hadith explains this:

> God Almighty says: "I have divided *Salah* (Daily Prayers) between Myself and My servant into two halves, and My servant will get what he asks for." When the servant says, "All praise is for God," God says, "My servant has praised Me." When he says, "*the All-Merciful, the All-Compassionate*," God says, "My servant has extolled Me." When he says, "*the Master of the Day of Judgment*," God says, "My servant has glorified Me and submitted to My power." When he says, "*You alone do We worship, and from You alone do we seek help*," God says, "This is between Me and My servant, and My servant will get what he has asked for." When he says, "*Guide us to the Straight Path, the path of those whom You have favored, not of those who have incurred Your wrath, nor of those who are astray*," God says, "This is for My servant, and My servant will get what he has asked for."[53]

When we recite Fatiha, we should pay attention to the Divine truth explained here. In reciting Fatiha, we ask God to guide us to the straight path which has been proved by all the Prophets and eminent friends of God, and God promises us to give us what we ask for. We should always remember that God has bestowed a great privilege upon us in the universe, so we should live accordingly.

* * *

Among the countless blessings of God is our existence itself: God brought us into being out of nothing. Then He directed our existence from finitude to infinity, our attention from multiplicity to unity. He held our hand in a realm that we would be lost otherwise and He lead us to the palaces of happiness in the world of Divine unity. He oriented our faces towards our origin and enraptured our hearts with the sacred word: "*We belong to God and to Him is our return*" (al-Baqarah 2:156). We originated in God's will and power, and we will turn back to Him. We will attain eternity in this way and find everlasting happiness. He has satisfied our hearts and honored us with these blessings.

---

[53] *Sahih Muslim*, Salah, 38; *Sunan at-Tirmidhi*, Tafsir *surah* 1, 1; *Sunan Abu Dawud*, Salah, 131.

Although all these gifts are given by God, they also relate to our will: We willingly exert effort to reach them. When we want to be guided, God will guide us in this world that good is mixed with evil, truth with falsity, faith with unbelief, angels with devils, the righteous with the unrighteous. God gave us willpower, a manifestation of His own will. Freewill is such a treasure that if it is misused, it brings trouble on its owner. We often misuse our will. Humanity has many times abused its free will, went beyond the limits, and assumed authority alongside God. As an example, the Pharaoh is told in the Qur'an to have proclaimed divinity over his people, saying, "I am your supreme lord!" (an-Naziat 79:24). He abused his willpower and stood against God's authority.

There is power in the universe alternative or complementary to God's authority. All existence testifies to God's unity. The Qur'an says:

$$\text{لَوْ كَانَ فِيهِمَا ءَالِهَةٌ إِلَّا اللهُ لَفَسَدَتَا}$$

Had there been in the heavens and the earth any deities other than God, both (of those realms) would certainly have fallen into ruin (al-Anbiya 21:22).

It is because God is the only creator that the universe is in order. To assume other deities is to assume the destruction of this universal order. God is the creator of everything in nature. He creates even our works: We see, hear, and breathe thanks to His creative providence. The Qur'an teaches:

$$\text{وَاللهُ خَلَقَكُمْ وَمَا تَعْمَلُونَ}$$

God creates you and all that you do (as-Saffat 37:96).

God granted us willpower to make our choices in life, but this does not mean that we are the creators of our lives. Since we are conscious and free under God's creative authority, we are morally responsible and accountable. This is why God warns us against evil and tells us that He will judge our deeds after death. He grants us temporal and relative power over our lives under His eternal and absolute authority, and advises us not to misuse this opportunity. Again, our willpower is a manifestation of God's special mercy and generosity upon us.

III.
"The Master of the Day of Judgment."

Out of His infinite mercy and generosity, God bestows upon us our humanity, our freedom and responsibility. It is so meaningful that this verse follows the previous one, linking Divine mercy to judgment. God is the Lord of the worlds, He is absolutely merciful and compassionate, and He is the only Master on the coming Day of Judgment. Originally, it is "the day of *deen*" and this word denotes both reward and punishment based on just judgment. Besides, the "Day" is the comprehensive period that covers the destruction of the universal order at the end of the world, the resurrection of the dead, and God's final judgment. *Deen* also means "religion," and in this case, the phrase tells that the Last Day will be the time for the true religion to be manifest to all people.

The principles of Islamic faith are indicated in the first three verses of Fatiha. Divine unity and our service to God are expressed in the verse: "All praise is for God, the Lord of the worlds." The Divine revelation by means of God's Messengers is implied in the verse: *"the All-Merciful, the All-Compassionate."* And the resurrection of the dead for the final judgment is taught by the verse: "The Master of the Day of Judgment." This is a great harmony. We are taught the whole of faith at once in a concise manner.

Divine unity requires our devotion and service. As God is absolutely merciful and compassionate, He revealed His guidance by sending to us Messengers and showing the straight path. And this guidance proves the coming of a day for a final judgment. On that day, God will manifest His mercy, generosity, and justice in an absolute way. He will punish the oppressors and reward the oppressed. The Divine blessings that we are allowed to taste a bit in this temporal world will continue permanently in the other, and this permanent grace will be the greatest manifestation of the Attributes: the Lord of the worlds, the All-Merciful, the All-Compassionate.

The Day of Judgment requires being both hopeful and fearful. We should be concerned with the final judgment and not feel as if we have already been saved. This is the way that the Qur'an and the Prophet, peace and blessings be upon him, teach us. In a *hadith qudsi*, God says: "I do not combine two confidences, nor do I combine two fears." Namely, if one is so confident in this world about his end, he will certainly fear in the Hereafter; and if he fears here about his end, he will be secured in the Hereafter. All people will witness this truth on the Day of Judgment.

1. The Day of Resurrection

On the Day of Resurrection, everybody will be raised from the dead. All deeds we do here in this world, good or evil, will be brought to be judged. And God Almighty will manifest His absolute authority. This is the meaning of "the Master of the Day of Judgment." In truth, God is the master of this world, too. But it is on the Day of Judgment that all people will fully understand God's absolute authority over everything.

To state again, the "Day" refers to the entire period in which the resurrection and the final judgment will be held. Just as our individual life time is divided in days, the life of a nation or community has its own days. In this figurative language, the world has its days through its life time. On the other hand, our entire life time in this world is called "today" or "the present day" compared to "the other day" or "the next day." Before God's glorious sovereignty, both this world and the next are just two days. All time is like an instant compared to His life. He is transcendent, above from time. When the present day will end, we will be judged of it on the next day. This world will be transformed into the next, and "*all secrets will be revealed*" (at-Tariq 86:90).

2. The Day of the Religion

As mentioned above, the original phrase for "the Day of Judgment" can be translated as "the day of the religion." This would mean that the truth of the Divine religion will be fully revealed on the Day of Resurrection. We believe in God, His angels, Books, and Messengers, and we believe in the final judgment and the Divine destiny. We also believe in the truth of *Salah*, the Daily Prayers, *Zakah*, the annual alms-giving, *Sawm*, the fasting in Ramadan, and *Hajj*, pilgrimage to Mecca. The truth of all these beliefs will be revealed on that day. Indeed, the whole of Islam, all truths that we are taught by the Qur'an and the Prophet, peace and blessings be upon him, will be revealed on the Day of Resurrection.

The religion of Islam is a Divine teaching. It is an order of life determined by God. Its origin and roots are in the Divine realm. As Islam manifests itself in this world, it will do the same in the Hereafter. Islam is God's law, *sharia*. It is a set of Divine rules that lead us to the good through our will. Islam does not negate our freedom. Humanity is not confined in the boundaries of its physical reality as other creatures are. As we are given free will, we make our choice between good and evil. This is why the traditional Islamic definition of "religion" emphasizes "guidance through our will."

A religion must be put by God, who absolutely knows what is good, who is absolutely capable to give us what He promises, and who can absolutely satisfy our mind and heart. Islam is such a religion. Those who replaced this Divine teaching with the abstract human conscience in our recent history made people bewildered with ways as many as the individual understandings. The rationalists who only trust in human reason could not understand our heart and soul. With the pure reason as their sole companion, they could not solve any essential problem of humanity. The intellect is an instrument to understand God's will manifested in the Divinely established religion.

The Divine religion addresses to all dimensions of human life. We are responsible to develop a full life for us by understanding God's will. The true religion should be applicable to all aspects of life. If we apply our religious values to our life for the ultimate purpose of God's good pleasure, no deeds in the name of piety will go in vain. The Qur'an teaches:

$$وَمَنْ يَعْمَلْ مِثْقَالَ ذَرَّةٍ شَرًّا يَرَهُ فَمَنْ يَعْمَلْ مِثْقَالَ ذَرَّةٍ خَيْرًا يَرَهُ$$

Whoever does an atom's weight of good will see it, and whoever does an atom's weight of evil will see it (az-Zalzalah 99:7–8).

If we expect something worldly in response to our piety, this means that we are insincere and that God will not accept our service. The only reason and goal of our service and piety should be God's command and good pleasure. A truly pious person expects God's reward in the Hereafter. The true religion is to live according to God's command and to hope His good pleasure in return.

3. The Word "Master"

The original word for "master" can be spelled in two ways. In the first case, the word is derived from *mulk* (sovereignty, dominion) and means ruler or king. In the second case, it is derived from *milk* (ownership) and means owner or master. The verse combines all these meanings.

The verse warns us about our temporal and relative ownership in the world. It seems as if the verse tells us: "You are given a relative ownership, but in the Hereafter, everything will absolutely belong to God. Then search for the ways to make your temporal ownership everlasting." God is the only owner of the world, and only the righteous are His "inheritors." We are God's vicegerents on earth and we should rule the land to represent His will of mercy and justice.

The verse also warns the rulers, especially the tyrants. It tells them: "Do not assume for you a lasting sovereignty! There will come a day on which you will totally lose everything you have. Remember that the only master on the Day of Judgment is God. So when you rule your nation, be aware of the limits of your authority compared to God's absolute one. If you think about the Divine rule while you work for the country, you can have a chance to be righteous. If you insist on injustice, you and your rule will be destroyed soon. Do not rely upon your power; rather rely upon God's power. If you trust in Him, He will restore your ownership in the Hereafter by granting you the everlasting life out of His infinite mercy and generosity."

In the course of the *surah*, we have first praised God, have witnessed God's absolute lordship and providence in the universe, understood that God guides everything in the creation towards perfection in a great plan that will end up with Hereafter. And now with this verse, we understand that God will bring a day to ultimately distinguish the good from the evil, the beautiful from the ugly. It is the time when the righteous will be unimaginably rewarded while the unrighteous will look for a place to hide. It is the day on which the truth of the Divine religion will be fully manifest. On that day, only God will speak and judge, only God will reward or punish. Therefore, as long as we live, we only need to turn to Him and nothing else.

IV.
"You alone do We worship,
and from You alone do we seek help."

We have arrived at the presence of God after all the studies and searches that lead to Him. It seems that the opening part of the *surah*, which is until this verse, has prepared us for this meeting. Entering His lofty presence, we display our service and say: "We worship only You, and we seek help only from You." We practice this in every *Salah* every day. The noble Prophet, peace and blessings be upon him, attracts our attention to the value of *Salah* when he says: "*Salah* is the believer's ascension to God's presence."[54] In our Daily Prayer, we present to God our service in different forms of showing respect and gratitude; we transcend the space and ascend a position between contingence and necessity, between temporality and eternity. It is a lofty position that we combine "being together with" and "being different from" God. How fortunate we are when we ascend this position five times a day, a relative position that the Prophet, peace and blessings be upon him, absolutely attained in his special heavenly journey.

1. Concept of Worship

The Arabic verb for "worship" is *ibada* and it has alternative lexical forms like *ubuda* and *ubudiyya*. These forms have nuances and they all denote to humble yourself before God, glorify and show respect to Him.

---

[54]   ar-Razi, Fakhruddin, *Mafatih al-Ghayb*, I, 214; Suyuti, *Sharh Sunan Ibn Majah*, 313.

It ideally means to solely and humbly turn to God, with our attention focused on His good pleasure. As believers, we admit our humility before His greatness. We present our service to Him in a discipline He taught us, not arbitrarily. With this presentation, we mean to say: "I am your servant and You are my Lord. I am a tiny thing wandering in this broad universe and You are the transcendent Lord of all worlds."

In Islamic law, *ibada* means the act of obedience to God that is done with the pure intention of being close to Him and receiving reward from Him. The meaning of closeness is necessary in the concept of worship. Pure intention is also a necessary condition for an act to be considered worship. We may study the universe and contemplate creation, but these acts are not worship until we direct our intention to God. Without such intention, such acts cannot bring us closer to God. This is true even about charity and recitation of the Qur'an: They can be considered worship only if pure intention accompanies them.

Worship is a disciplined act of orientation towards God, and we should orient to Him the whole of our mind, conscience, heart, our internal and external senses, and our tongue. Only God is worthy of worship and this is emphasized in the sentence: "You alone do we worship." We may show respect to others, but this is not an act of worship. True worship reveals our poverty, impotence, weakness, and even nothingness before God. It is the embodied awareness that all our happiness and prosperity lies in closeness to God.

* * *

Let us now approach the concept of worship by psychological analysis. Our soul is a station for hopes, loves, pains, and grieves. We are always suspicious about things which may cause pain. We do not like such things and keep away from them. We even feel angry of them. On the other hand, we are fond of things that cause pleasure. We are bound to them with hope and ambition. We also maintain a balance between worry and hope, fear and joy. When we feel hopeless, we lose our desire to work, resorting to sloth. If people in society are fearless, they will likely act irresponsibly. Having no worry or concern will cause us to exceed moral boundaries.

This is why God gave us a nature that harbors fear and hope. We naturally love beauty and we fear the threats hidden in future. At times, our fear overwhelms our hope; we are terrified with the idea of a final judgment. A balanced version of this consideration is necessary to sustain justice in a community. But if fear is misused, it distorts our life. We are terrified by countless things like earthquake, comets, snakes, and germs. There can be no peace in this situation.

Love is also a trial. At times we love things which do not stay loyal to our feelings: They do not recognize our love or they leave us even without a good wish. Our love of youth, power, and beauty is like this. Many times our beloved ones treat us the same way. This means that even love can be a trouble. Love may make us blind and deaf. We may not see even the obvious facts about our relationship with the things we are fond of. We should love them with recognition of the temporal nature of having them.

When misused, both love and fear can make us servants to those which or whom we love or fear. This is totally against the principle of Divine unity. We produce many deities in this way. But we definitely lose when our heart is bound to temporal concerns. We will never attain what we falsely hope: Either we will leave them or they will. The Messenger of God, peace and blessings be upon him, was a special beloved for his companions, the Muslims of the early Islam. They profoundly loved him with pure hearts. But when he passed away, these companions did not act any ways against the principle of Divine unity. For they truly understood the truth that only God is immortal. Just some individuals lost their faith since they had not shared this understanding.

When the Prophet, peace and blessings be upon him, fulfilled his duties perfectly and completed his mission, he accepted the invitation of his Lord and moved towards the eternal realm. People were so sad. Umar ibn al-Khattab, one of those with pure faith in Divine unity, was among those who were shaken. He even claimed that the Prophet did not die. But Abu Bakr was more conscious. Upon hearing the sad news, he came to the Prophet's home, kissed his face, and said: "Your death is as beautiful as your life. You have died once and will never die any-more." Then he moved to the mosque, where the companions were seat-ed in sorrow. He climbed the pulpit and recited the following verse that suddenly awakened the people:

وَمَا مُحَمَّدٌ إِلَّا رَسُولٌ قَدْ خَلَتْ مِنْ قَبْلِهِ الرُّسُلُ أَفَإِنْ مَاتَ أَوْ قُتِلَ انْقَلَبْتُمْ عَلَى أَعْقَابِكُمْ وَمَنْ يَنْقَلِبْ عَلَى عَقِبَيْهِ فَلَنْ يَضُرَّ اللهَ شَيْئًا وَسَيَجْزِي اللهُ الشَّاكِرِينَ

Muhammad is but a Messenger, and Messengers passed away before him. If, then, he dies or is killed, will you turn back on your heels? Whoever turns back on his heels can in no way harm God. But God will abundantly reward the thankful ones (Al Imran 3:144).

The companions were awakened at that moment and fully under-stood that the Prophet had gone and the Divine revelation had stopped. They understood the verse in such a new way that as if it was revealed at that moment. In fact, the verse had been revealed several years ago, following the Battle of Uhud, and they had recited it many times in the meantime. But they had not been able to comprehend its meaning as deeply as Abu Bakr had done. The verse reminded them that the Proph-et, peace and blessings be upon him, completed his work in this tem-poral world but God is always alive and works. In this way, Abu Bakr managed to make the people calm down and escape hesitations.[55]

Now that even the Messenger of God, peace and blessings be upon him, is not to be loved as if he is immortal, then we should check our loves directed to many tiny idols. We should correct them with our faith in Divine unity. When we devote ourselves to mortal beloveds, we start to live in a dual mode. We invent new deities that make trou-bles in our life. But if we really know that the ultimate object of our love should be solely God, we will find the true peace and happiness.

Our soul inherently tends towards God. God placed in us the strong feelings of love and fear, and they will lead us to peace and happiness if we direct them to their true object. As a child takes refuge in his mother even when he fears her punishment, we appeal to God at the

---

[55]   Ibn Sa'd, *At-Tabaqat al-Kubra*, II, 266–272; Abd ar-Razzaq, *Al-Musannaf*, V, 433–437.

same time that we fear Him. We find a limitless spiritual pleasure not only in the love but also the fear of God. The true worship to God requires both love and fear. True service is a balanced mixture of these apparently opposing feelings. In our service, we feel that our love and fear of God are waving like an ocean without shore in us along a wind of infinite peace.

Those who do not understand their own humility and impotence cannot understand the true nature of worship. They are unfortunate in this regard. The spirit of worship demands humility, hope, and fear. Worry and joy intermingle in it. You can be sure that you are in God's presence if you have combined this worry and joy. If you have set the balance of fear and hope, this means you have attained true peace. However, this peace is out of reach for those arrogant who do not fear God and are cheerfully sure of their future, or for those desperate who give up hope of God's infinite mercy and generosity.

* * *

Intention is the spirit of worship. Our worship should be moderate and balanced and in conformity with the principles God set. Among these principles is the purity of intention. It is essential to our service. No ritual can be considered worship without pure intention. In a hadith, the Prophet, peace and blessings be upon him, says:

> "Perhaps a fasting person obtains nothing from his fasting but hunger and one who stands during the night in prayer nothing but tiredness."[56]

By "intention" we mean that our heart should be oriented to God only. Without this orientation, even charity cannot be considered a truly religious act. If God is not our purpose, all our work to spread the good in society might be some deceptive dialectics and demagogies. A struggle for religion is not but a show, a waste of time and money, if God is not the purpose. The goal of an act of worship must be solely God's good pleasure. Turning to God sincerely is the soul of worship.

---

[56] *Sunan Ibn Majah*, Siyam, 21; Darimi, Riqaq, 12.

In his sincere worship, a servant seems to say: "I have come to Your presence, admitting my humility before Your glory. While I never bow before anyone else, I humbly bow before You. I destroy my pride with the spirit of my prostration with my face on the ground. For You are God and I am servant; You are the Creator and I am a creature. I have come to Your presence by admitting my poverty. You have given me mind, will, and conscience. My soul wants to express its gratitude and praise to You. Let the entire universe be witness that I am Your humble servant and this service is my honor."

We feel and think this way when we say, "You alone do we worship." This is the way to attain the true greatness, the greatest position that is indicated in *shahada* when we say: "And I bear witness that Muhammad is God's servant and Messenger." He is a servant first of all, and his service is permanent. He had been God's servant before his mission, and this service increased by his mission. When he died, his mission ceased, but his service kept going on.

We never give up our freedom even if we were offered the world. We never accept to be servant to anyone else than God. We are willing to give away our soul for God's sake, who created us and made us feel His existence. We can face up to all fears and can sacrifice all other loves in His cause. We know that we will win Him even if we lose everything else. We prefer serving God in this world with our sweat and tear to a life in a paradise. We enthusiastically and sincerely undertake a task that would overwhelm the mountains. This is the Divine "trust" of service mentioned in the following verse:

إِنَّا عَرَضْنَا الْأَمَانَةَ عَلَى السَّمَوَاتِ وَالْأَرْضِ وَالْجِبَالِ فَأَبَيْنَ أَنْ يَحْمِلْنَهَا وَأَشْفَقْنَ مِنْهَا وَحَمَلَهَا الْإِنْسَانُ إِنَّهُ كَانَ ظَلُومًا جَهُولًا

We offered the Trust to the heavens, and the earth, and the mountains, but they shrank from bearing it, and were afraid of it, but man has undertaken it. But he is indeed prone to doing great wrong and misjudging, and acting out of sheer ignorance (al-Ahzab 33:72).

2. The Concept of Seeking Help

The words and sentences of the Qur'an flow so harmoniously and consistently. When the Qur'an informs us about the heavy responsibility of worship, it teaches us how to fulfill this task and sheds light on our way. This teaching corresponds to the fact that we ask God for help in the matter of worship and say: "And from You alone do we seek help." Asking God for help in any matter, be it worldly or otherworldly, is called *isti'ana*, a term that is derived from this verse in Fatiha. This pious act is strongly emphasized in the Prophetic tradition.[57]

God's help is two kinds: necessary and voluntary. The former is manifested in our special creation with such a blessed composition of body and soul. Each of our natural abilities is this kind: we see, hear, smell, touch, taste, think, and understand thanks to God's creative grace. The second kind of help is manifested in God's guidance and providence in the course of our life. We act and work with the abilities that God created for us and with the providence He bestows upon us. Even the most ordinary human acts come to existence under God's authority, although we exert our will through them. But our first creation is completely necessary and compulsory. God did not ask us about the principles of the creation of this world. God set them by Himself. As a part of these principles, He granted us free will, making us responsible for our deeds.

God teaches us how to turn to Him and gives us the right to ask Him for help in this matter. He promises to respond to our prayers. We work and ask for help, and He creates and helps. Every work of us has a relation to God's will. Our works come into existence as a creation of God in an ultimate sense. Our work is also His work in this sense, and this relation is a great honor for us. This understanding does not allow fatalism or its opposite, the denial of Divine determination.

Let me explain this balanced understanding. The subject is called *qadar* (Divine destiny or predestination) in Islamic terminology. Things exist in God's knowledge before God creates them with His will and power. God's foreknowledge does not necessitate the existence of the

---

57   Tabari, *Jami al-Bayan*, I, 69; Ibn Abi Hatim, *At-Tafsir*, I, 29.

things. God creates our acts and works according to our voluntary choice. *Qadar* denotes this Divine foreknowledge, which includes our voluntary choices. Even the fact that this foreknowledge was recorded in the Divine book of destiny does not force us to act or work in a certain way. Then we do not need to accept the claims of Mutazila and Jabriyya, the two extreme theological schools that hold the denial of predestination and fatalism respectively.

This understanding of Divine destiny perfectly explains the truth of the following verse of Fatiha: "Guide us to the straight path." This prayer indicates the beautiful relationship between God and the servant. In a sense, this prayer is the expression of the agreement or testament between God and the servant which is held in the verse: "You alone do we worship and from You alone do we seek help." Namely, we will serve God and He will help us. This agreement is the loftiest honor for humanity. It is greater than being a king of a country, for God is the King who owns and rules everything in the universe including our souls.

God rules the universe with His title: the Lord of the worlds. Through His providence, He guides everything in creation towards perfection. For His Names *Rahman* and *Rahim*, He made the earth a great feast for humanity. He equipped our body with functions that perfectly match this feast. In this way, God introduced Himself to us as the All-Merciful and the All-Compassionate. Then He made us feel His absolute authority with the verse, "*the Master of the Day of Judgment.*" Thus He encouraged us to be prepared for tomorrow. Through His guidance, He bestowed upon us a way of life that is in conformity with the life to come.

* * *

The verse: "*You alone do we worship and from You alone do we seek help,*" strengthen the sense of community among us, for we say "we" instead of "I." The congregational prayer is the symbol of the order and coherence of our community. If we feel the true sense of communal life in our prayer, this will be reflected in the social practice. As our mutual stance before God shows it, "we" are a harmonious community with a unified soul, not a crowd.

This consideration saves us from a selfish life and elevates us to the heights of a logical and rational way of life; it makes us a living member of the society. However, this enlightenment depends on the degree of the depth of our conscience. A society composed of those with deep conscience will be firmly established, stable, and unshakable. As for those with shallow conscience, they are not able to establish a society. Such people comprise a crowd. A true community is the one of deep conscience and its shared soul is represented in the communal prayer. This is why it is strongly recommended in Islamic law to practice the daily prayers in congregation.

The Qur'an instructs the principles of a true society and teaches us how to attain it. The Qur'an educates the individuals to this end, a Divine training that is to be carried out by the hands of God's Messengers and the scholars who follow them. Getting unified in time under the same moral authority and a single social contract, individuals start to behave as if they are the organs of the same body. If a society lacks this unification, its people necessarily suffer from confrontations and dispersion. Unless we are unified in mind and heart, we cannot form a coherent society.

With this verse and others, the Qur'an advises us to say "we" in the place of "I" and prepares us for a unified community. It ensures us that the morally perfect individuals will cause new formations in society. The leaders will emerge among such ideal individuals in a natural and almost spontaneous way. To say again, only a Prophetic tradition of education can make such ideal people possible. The Prophet, peace and blessings be upon him, has the deepest conscience. The Qur'an tells that God expanded his heart (ash-Sharh 94:1). So he opened his heart and bosom so much that he treated even the worst behaviors with tolerance, showing the ways to a true community. His example proves that even a small community can play a historic role in the destiny of humanity thanks to its members with deep conscience.

A society grows by the merit of conscience, and one formed of stiff hearts cannot survive. It is the deep conscience that makes a society securely founded. Any people of good intention can easily find a place in such a society. It is surely an enormous task to found this society;

but once founded, it lives so long and plays a great role in history. God's Prophets have proved this. The Prophet, peace and blessings be upon him, was the first and best building block of his society, and his companions followed his example in a best way. We hope that God will expand the conscience of our community and make us the true followers of the Qur'an. Then we can contribute to humanity greatly, open the congested ways of sciences, and help humanity attain the true horizons of both material and spiritual prosperity. We hope these from the infinite mercy of our Lord.

Those selfish ones who prioritize their desires and want all others to think like them cannot establish a stable society. On the other hand, those tolerant ones who appreciate all ways that help reach the truth are always able to found a long-lasting society. The verse inspires us this tolerance when it teaches us to transcend our personal ego. It teaches us to offer our worship to God in a communal context, thinking: "O my Lord! My personal worship is so little, but I am among these people who serve You. Thousands of communities are now worshipping You on earth. Even the molecules in my body, all plants and animals in nature, and all angels in the heavens are worshipping You. I am offering my worship in the midst of all these worships. I believe that I cannot live except in a community where I can say 'us' in the place of 'me.' Here I am following the imam like other members of the community, as You created us with a 'social' nature. We are following his recitation to be harmonious in the prayer."

* * *

We find a strong sense of Divine unity in the verse: "You alone do we worship and from You alone do we seek help." Up until this verse, Fatiha has taught us that God is the only Divine authority and He is the Lord of the worlds who governs the universe through His all-encompassing providence. The Names "the All-Merciful" and "the All-Compassionate" have told us that God provides for everything in the world, from the infant in the womb to the insect in the cocoon. So we have clearly understood what we always witness Divine unity in the clear face of creation.

As our unique Lord, God has given us whatever we have gained in our life. We have received all things from Him. So we should recognize Him as our only Lord. We should keep our spiritual attention away from anyone else. With the spirit of a sincere address to God with a "You," we can attain what is called the unity of worship, a necessary consequence of Divine unity. We should say: "O my Lord! As You have put everything in the universe in my service, I am at Your service, listening to Your commands. I live with Your providence, and this is my honor and joy." This unity of worship is our response to Divine unity.

Unfortunately, a great part of humanity does not understand this unity, so they worship many things in nature. Deprived of the true pleasure of worshipping God Almighty, they follow many false deities only to be disappointed and desolated on the way or at the end of the day. All praise be to God who has guided us by the Qur'an and the Prophet to Divine unity and the unity of worship. All thanks be to God who has not left us lost in such a universe.

V.
"Guide us to the Straight Path."

S ervice to God is a profound task. We cannot fulfill it with our personal, individual effort. Only within a community can we offer to God a service that His glory requires. In this sense, with a plural language, we ask God for guidance: "Guide us to the straight path." This prayer is so comprehensive, for "guidance" relates to all aspects of life. We cannot put in order our personal, familial, and societal life without God's guidance.

If we analyze or examine the human soul with the metaphysical principles set by humanity, if we attempt to understand ourselves, our virtues and weaknesses without reference to the principles taught by Divine revelation, the results will always be flawed and incomplete. If we accept the Divine guidance in this matter, we will understand the truth of our human reality and find it fully illumined. We should also regulate our family and social life according to the Divine principles. God is the only authority that can enable us to establish a true agreement in society. Without God, society is destined to destructive disagreements.

1. The Meaning of Guidance

Divine guidance is God's sufficient response to our countless needs. The phrase "guide us" is a prayer and supplication. The plural language means that we want for others what we want for ourselves. *Hidaya* or "guidance" means to lead someone gently to the goal. True guidance is the one that makes us reach the purpose. God shows us the straight path that leads to the paradise; He kindly holds our hands and does not leave us alone with our misleading desires. In fact, "guide us" does not mean "show us." For guidance denotes that the Guide is with us during the way to help us until we reach the final destination.

Divine guidance may come directly or by some means. At times, people are lost despite all favorable conditions. And at other times, we find our way despite all unfavorable conditions. Prophet Noah's son did not benefit from his closeness to the Divine guidance, although Prophets Abraham and Moses became God's Messengers even though they grew in the house of two unbelievers. As the Qur'an states, God brings forth the living out the dead and brings the dead out of the living (Al Imran 3:27; al-An'am 6:95).

God has guided us endlessly. First, He granted us harmony between our physical and spiritual existence. In essence, our body and spirit are from different worlds and their desires and tendencies are different from each other. But God united these differences in a great whole, and this unity is the unique way to our happiness. All faculties of our unified existence should follow God's guidance in order to maintain its original unity. If any of them exceeds its boundaries, the unity will be broken and happiness will be out of reach. Besides, God showed us the true as distinct from the wrong. In the Qur'an, God says: "*Have we not shown him the two ways?*" (al-Balad 90:10). God gave us the ability to distinguish the true from the wrong, the good from the evil. God also says: "*Those who strive hard for Our sake, We will most certainly guide them to Our ways*" (al-Ankabut 29:69), and these ways have been shown by God's Messengers and Books. The Qur'an explains: "*This Qur'an surely guides to that which is most just and right*" (al-Isra 17:9). "*We made them leaders, guiding people by Our command*" (al-Anbiya 21:73).

God guides us endlessly throughout the entire process of our coming into existence and throughout our life. We transcended many levels of existence, from the realm of molecules to that of animals, up to the realm of humanity, and we ourselves did not do anything for this long existential journey. We found ourselves at where we are. God guided us throughout this journey. In our life, He guides us through different ways, especially by revelation and inspiration. He even shows us some signs of truth in our dreams. God's greatest guidance is manifested in the religion of Islam, the only straight path among many twisted ones. While millions of others, more intelligent than us, wander without a true direction, God honored us with guiding us to Islam and making us follow the noblest of humanity, Prophet Muhammad, peace and blessings be upon him,. And we celebrate God's praises in response to all these blessings.

2. The Word "Path"

The definite article in the phrase "the straight path" (*as-sirat al-mustaqim*) denotes that the path for which we ask guidance is a well-known one. It is the path that millions of righteous and virtuous people have walked on before us: God's Prophets and all true followers of them. This well-known "path" is the way that leads us to God's good pleasure. It is straight but there are trials on it. It is not so easy to walk on. And this "path" reminds us of the way that extends over the Hell to the Paradise which all people will be forced to walk through.

There are other words in Arabic that are synonymous to the word *sirat* (path) such as *sabil* and *tariq*. Likewise, there are alternatives for the adjective *mustaqim* (straight) like *mustawi*. In order to truly understand what God means in this verse, we need to pay attention to these nuances. The selection of these words is not arbitrary, for the Qur'an is absolutely wise. As God created the universe with infinite wisdom, He revealed the Qur'an the same way. Many verses indicate this fact, such as: "*This is the Book being sent down in parts from God, the All-Glorious, the All-Wise*" (al-Jathiyah 45:2). In particular, we should linguistically analyze the phrase "the straight path" in order to understand God's intentions with it concerning our personal and communal "way" of life.

In traditional commentaries, "the straight path" is explained as the moderate, middle, true way, which is the entirety of Islam, or the whole of Islamic law, which is ideally exemplified by the Prophet, peace and blessings be upon him, and his companions. It is also associated with the way between the place of the Final Judgment and Paradise, which is like a bridge extending over the Hell. In a hadith, the Prophet, peace and blessings be upon him, says that the straight path is God's book, namely the Qur'an.[58] In this sense, when we say, "Guide us to the straight path," we ask God to guide us to the truths He teaches us in the Qur'an. In another hadith, the Prophet, peace and blessings be upon him, defines the Qur'an as follows: "It is the strong rope of God. It is the wise reminder. It is the straight path."[59]

God's Messenger, peace and blessings be upon him, is reported to have said:

> "God explains to you the straight path with this example: There are walls at both sides of the road and there are opened gates on the walls with curtains covering them. A man standing on the road calls: 'O people, go on the straight path and do not disperse!' If any of them wants to lift the curtain and open the gate, another man warns the passengers, saying: 'Stop! Do not open it, for if you do that, you will get out of the way.' Now, the road is Islam. The two walls are the boundaries that God has set in the religion. The opened gates are the things that God has forbidden. The calling person is God's book. And the warning person is conscience, the advisor that God put in the heart of every believer."[60]

Conscience discerns the bad aspects in the things God forbids, and it always dislikes them. It is only conscience that can feel the sufferings of an unbelieving heart. One will hear the painful voice of his conscience when he steps into unbelief or any wrong way. The above hadith teaches us that we should listen to the voice of the Qur'an and our conscience. We should walk straight on God's path under the light of His revelation without lifting the curtains of the gates which lead to the forbidden acts.

The moderate or middle way, the true way, the religion of Islam or the Islamic law: all denotations of the phrase "the straight path" correspond to each other. Islam is a straight path, moderate and middle, away from extremes. Islam is the straightest and truest way, for it is the sum

---

58 Ibn Abi Hatim, *At-Tafsir*, I, 30.

59 *Sunan at-Tirmidhi*, Fadail al-Qur'an, 14; Darimi, *Fadail al-Qur'an*, 1.

60 Ahmad ibn Hanbal, *Al-Musnad*, IV, 182; Tabarani, *Musnad ash-Shamiyyin*, III, 177.

of God's rules. To seek alternative "straight" or "true" ways proves one's confusion about the meaning of "straight" and "true." Islam is the manifest way that leads us to the absolute good, which is our ultimate goal. The way of Islam is both theoretical and practical, both physical and spiritual.

When we say, "From You alone do we seek help," we ask God for help in an absolute sense, and then we make this "help" particular when we ask for guidance to the straight path. The harmony between these two verses makes us feel the peace that Islam promises, and it also shows us the deep meaning of asking from God.

In reality, all ways come from God and return to Him. There is no path in the universe that does not originate in God's creation and turn to His presence. All pathways in nature and society are the manifestations of Divine principles. Nonetheless, some ways are open to misuse and hence illegitimate actions. In this regard, some ways lead to God's good pleasure whereas some others lead to God's wrath. All laws of nature and society are set by God. We can discover these laws by scientific study but we do not invent them. We find and recognize them, but this does not make us lawmaker, which is only God, who set all pathways in the universe in a great complexity and harmony.

* * *

Our body is composed of many materials with pleasant or unpleasant look. But all these materials complementarily function in a great order. Likewise, we have many feelings that comprise our spiritual existence, some of which may look evil, such as lust, anger, and hatred. But even these apparently evil feelings are functional in a great spiritual order and they can be utilized for good purposes. If we did not have any desire, we would not want to eat or sleep, or get married and have children, and this would mean the demise of humanity. On the other extreme, one is so obedient to his desires that he does not recognize any moral boundaries. He lifts the curtains mentioned in the hadith to violate God's laws and gets out of the moderate way of the mainstream humanity.

The "straight path" is moderate and away from extremes. Those who adopt this way will dislike the immoral and illegitimate acts, being contented with the permitted things. They will even abstain from suspicious things in case they may be prohibited. They are the believing servants of God. They keep their feelings balanced: neither dead nor excessive. For instance, they control their anger in the face of bothering events, but this does not prevent them from the recognition of their responsibility. Instead, they know how to utilize their anger in the cause of justice. They are not like those who do not feel anything against injustice, nor like those who make everything victims to their fury. The life of the Prophet, peace and blessings be upon him, is the best manifestation of this virtue of balance. For he is the best to seek help from God and ask God for guidance.

The balance of the power of intellect is another example. One extreme is consistent speculation and dialectic, which many times misguide or deceive masses. The other extreme is the lack of reasoning and understanding. Those of moderate intellect will say: "Examine my words. If they are wrong, just disregard them." Being so modest, they show the true meaning of logic and being rational. They are away from the both extremes. They are on the straight path that we believers ask for at least forty times a day in our prayers.

The sense of "nature" should be balanced, too. We are part of nature, the fruit of this magnificent tree of creation. We are physically made of natural materials, but we also transcend the boundaries of nature with our spiritual dimension. One extreme in this matter is naturalism, namely seeing nature the ultimate source of existence. If we search everything in nature, we will be naturalist. Materialism emerges in this kind of view. From its ancient to contemporary forms, naturalism argues for a natural life, living in accordance with the laws of nature and disregarding all rules "invented" by people including religion. In fact, naturalism is a delusion and deviation. We live in nature but our spiritual life is not bound to the physical aspects of the world. On the other hand, the opposite extreme is to abandon nature totally or even to be against nature. As witnessed in sophistic skepticism and ascetic mysticism, such view is a neglect of the laws of the Divine creation.

Generally, the proponents of this view are defeated by these laws at the end of the day.

God set a balanced relationship between humanity and nature. We should observe this balance not to be dragged to the extremes. Many times, one extreme attitude causes its opposite to emerge. We can be saved from such immoderate positions when we follow the "straight path," the path of the Prophet, peace and blessings be upon him, and his companions. Umar ibn al-Khattab was one of those companions who perfectly understood the Divine laws in creation. As a caliph, he knew well how to govern a country. He was also a soldier, one who struggled in the cause of Islam, and a devout worshipper, a sincere servant of God. Wise enough, he had a balanced relationship with the natural world. He had a family and followed a moderate dietary; and he did not take the material dimension of life as his purpose. When he traveled to Damascus, a place under his rule, the saddle of the camel ripped his trousers, and he sewed it by himself. That time, he was the ruler of a country twenty times larger than Turkey. He was a man of balance, a man of the straight path.

* * *

We should ask God for guidance at all time and concerning all matters of life. We need to practice this in such a flowing and changing course of life. In fact, we Muslims do so in our dairy prayer. Every day, we turn to the Ka'ba many times, standing behind God's Messenger in our imagination, and pray to God, saying: "Guide us to the straight path." Although we are already guided to faith, we over and again ask God for guidance.

This consistent asking for guidance signifies the fact that "guidance" is by different degrees. In another words, the prayer "guide us" means different things according to the positions of the asking persons. If one is a sinner, the guidance is for sincere faith and righteousness. If he has faith, the guidance is for perfect faith, one that is deepened with wisdom. If he has perfect faith, the guidance is for the persistence of this position until death.

Many times we are engaged with thoughts and words which are against our faith, and this injures our soul and heart. Our imagination often falls into immorality and drags our soul into it, seriously damaging our lofty feelings and spiritual abilities. This fact proves that we need to ask for guidance every day in order to remove the dirt and dust from our heart and soul. In saying, "Guide us to the straight path," we admit our faults and mistakes, ask God forgiveness for our past, and ask Him for help of the future.

The straight path passes through a world that is a mixture of the right and wrong. To proceed on the straight path requires knowing both the right and wrong. It demands protecting our life from the wrong and keeping the right alive as much as we can. The religious commandments regulate our procession through the way. With negative commandments, God prohibits wrong acts, explains the reason behind the prohibitions, and determines a punishment for them. With positive commandments, God prescribes the right acts and encourages us for them. These two kinds comprise the Islamic law.

VI.

"The Path of those whom You have favored, not of those who have incurred (Your) wrath, nor of those who are astray."

We live on Divine favors and blessings. God bestows upon us what we need and what we delight, and in this way He manifests His lordship over humanity. God's greatest blessing is Islam, for it meets our greatest needs and we feel the greatest spiritual pleasures in it. Unfortunately, there are many who are born and live in an Islamic context but do not benefit from this greatest blessing. They do not hear God's Name that is loudly proclaimed many times every day from the minarets. There are many like some relatives of the Prophet, peace and blessings be upon him, who are not able to receive a single flash from the torch lit in their home.

The world is so complicated that only God can take care of everything in it. He is the only One who bestows upon creatures what they need every day. No human authority can manage to supply these needs. God's authority is all-encompassing over nature, and He provides for all at the same time. We need God's providence to be guided, and we feel this need deeply when we say: "*The path of those whom You have favored.*" Our needs are countless and thus God's favors and blessings are countless. Without His providence, these needs are definitely out of reach for us. He creates them and makes them available.

God's favors and blessings can be categorized in different ways. Some are worldly and some otherworldly. Some are given directly and some require our work. Some are spiritual and some material. Among them is the great blessing of "life," which enables us to interact with the entire earth unlike inanimate creatures as they are fixed in a certain location. The human life is God's special grace upon us. And our intellect and conscience are the most precious manifestations of this special grace. Besides, we cannot express how much beautiful it is that we are able to see, hear, taste, smell, and touch. And God gives us uncountable blessings available for these senses. Most of Divine blessings are given directly, without any work required from us. What is always required is our service to God, giving our thanks and showing deep respect to Him. We are expected to ask God for His favor and blessings and then thank Him sincerely.

God forgives us for our errors like neglecting His service, our arrogance, and our misuse of the abilities He has bestowed upon us. His forgiveness is a great favor and it more relates to the otherworld. Likewise, God prepares our heart for faith, prepares the Paradise for our eternal life, and puts in our soul an endless desire for this eternal life. Moreover, we passionately wish to witness His infinite beauty in Paradise. This endless desire and strong wish inherently originate in God's special creation. There cannot be any other origin for it. Thanks to this privileged creation, when "*God invites to the Abode of Peace*" (Yunus 10:25), we understand this call and feel deep enthusiasm.

We should contemplate all these Divine favors and blessings when we ask for guidance to "*the path of those whom You have favored.*" In reality, God's favors cannot be fully contemplated and appreciated. We often forget to thank God, for instance, for His great favor of living in a well-organized, stable society, in which we have opportunity to attain knowledge and morality. Freedom is another example for the great blessings that we are unable to appreciate truly. And our freedom gains its true meaning and value in our service to God. We are truly liberated when we truly serve God. In Rumi's words:

I have become a servant, become a servant, become a servant.
I have bowed to You and doubled myself over.
Slaves rejoice when they are emancipated;
Whereas I rejoice when I become Your servant.

God made us free when He bound us to Himself. To be bound to other creatures means desperate captivity and slavery. In this sense, we are truly free only under the Divine laws, and any other systems of law will restrict or destroy our freedom. Again, we believe that the true freedom is only possible in service to God. In the lack of this service, many false deities will emerge to captivate us. Most people in our time suffer from such captivity. Modern societies are typically deprived of the true sense of freedom and liberty. In fact, we have not appreciated the Divine gift of freedom and He has deprived us from it.

* * *

According to an alternative reading, the "straight path" is the Divine favor itself that God has bestowed upon the favored people. And these favored people are the best of humanity, the millions of enlightened souls that have passed through the true path of God before us. A verse in the Qur'an explains who these fortunate people are:

وَمَنْ يُطِعِ اللهَ وَالرَّسُولَ فَأُولَئِكَ مَعَ الَّذِينَ أَنْعَمَ اللهُ عَلَيْهِمْ مِنَ النَّبِيِّينَ
وَالصِّدِّيقِينَ وَالشُّهَدَاءِ وَالصَّالِحِينَ وَحَسُنَ أُولَئِكَ رَفِيقًا

Whoever obeys God and the Messenger, then those are (and in the Hereafter will be, in Paradise) in the company of those whom God has favored (with the perfect guidance): the Prophets, and the truthful ones (loyal to God's cause and truthful in whatever they do and say), and the witnesses (those who see the hidden Divine truths and testify thereto with their lives), and the righteous ones (in all their deeds and sayings, and dedicated to setting everything right). How excellent they are for companions! (an-Nisa 4:69).

This verse shows that the leaders on the straight path are God's Prophets, peace and blessings be upon them all. They are the stars in the sky of humanity. The Prophet, peace and blessings be upon him, met them in a spiritual encounter throughout his heavenly journey. When we come to the mosque to pray, we should remember how lofty and illuminated a group of people we follow. Moreover, this verse reminds us that we can attain the same fortune, the same privilege. Namely, when the next generations recite Fatiha and say, *"Guide us to the straight path, the path of those whom You have favored,"* we can be included in the referred people. This opportunity makes us excited and reminds us the serious task of leaving a good legacy behind. Only then can we benefit endlessly from the prayers of the coming generations.

* * *

The verse means that the people of the straight path are saved from God's wrath as they are not astray. But this does not mean that sincere believers are saved from adversities in this world. Instead, the world is a place of trial for all and hardships are typical means of the Divine test. Therefore, not all afflictions and calamities denote God's wrath. The Qur'an explains this as follows:

وَلَنَبْلُوَنَّكُمْ بِشَيْءٍ مِنَ الْخَوْفِ وَالْجُوعِ وَنَقْصٍ مِنَ الْأَمْوَالِ وَالْأَنْفُسِ وَالثَّمَرَاتِ
وَبَشِّرِ الصَّابِرِينَ الَّذِينَ إِذَا أَصَابَتْهُمْ مُصِيبَةٌ قَالُوا إِنَّا لِلَّهِ وَإِنَّا إِلَيْهِ رَاجِعُونَ

We will certainly test you with something of fear and hunger, and loss of wealth and lives and fruits (earnings); but give glad tidings to the persevering and patient: those who, when a disaster befalls them, say, "Surely we belong to God, and surely to Him we are bound to return." (al-Baqarah 2:155–156).

As long as we sincerely turn to God, all adversities and afflictions will turn into God's mercy upon us. Concerning this fact, the blessed Prophet, peace and blessings be upon him, says:

How amazing is the affair of the believer. Everything is good for him, and that is for no one but the believer: If good times come his way, he is thankful, and that is good for him; and if hardship comes his way, he is patient, and that is good for him.[61]

---

[61] *Sahih Muslim*, Zuhd, 64.

In addition, we can say that God's wrath is not totally contrary to His mercy, for God shows mercy even when He acts as if He is angry. All punishments prescribed against crimes in Islamic law can be considered in this kind. Behind the apparent wrath of the Lawmaker in these punishments, the regulations are due to His mercy upon all individuals in society. God combines His mercy and wrath in the same law.

* * *

There can be many different causes for going astray. Diverging from or losing completely the true way will result in confusion, lack of confidence, bewilderment, and fear. Those who are astray cannot see the bright face of the truth. So when we say, *"Nor of those who are astray,"* we take refuge in God and ask Him to protect us from losing the straight path.

Grammatically, the Arabic phrases for *"those who have incurred Your wrath"* and *"those who are astray"* refer to all possible people in these categories in all times.

* * *

The word *"amin"* (amen) is a request and it means "Accept my prayer." It is a strong Prophetic tradition to say this word at the end of the recitation of Fatiha. It is reported that the Prophet, peace and blessings be upon him, said:

> "When the imam says 'amin,' follow him and say 'amin.' For if your 'amin' coincides with the 'amin' of the angels, your previous wrong actions will be forgiven."[62]

It is also reported that whenever the Prophet, peace and blessings be upon him, said "amin" together with the congregation standing behind him, it was as if the mosque was shaken.[63]

---

[62] *Sahih al-Bukhari*, Adhan, 111, 113; *Sahih Muslim*, Salah, 72.
[63] *Sunan Ibn Majah*, Iqama, 14.

Summary

T he Qur'an contains the essential teachings of God's previous
revelations. Similarly, the *surah* of Fatiha contains the essential messages of the entire Qur'an. The words and verses of
the Qur'an are harmoniously related to each other, and the *surah* of
Fatiha perfectly exemplifies this fact. Fatiha is so coherent in linguistic, artistic, and conceptual terms that it looks like a single verse. If a
verse is a reason, the following one is its consequence. The seven
verses explain one another.

"All praise is for God, the Lord of the worlds." This short sentence
displays a strong harmony. If we ask why all praise is for God, the
answer is: For He is the Lord of the worlds. He is the unique Lord of
humanity. All praise is for God because He created us in such an excellent form and bestowed upon us such a spiritual stature. He raised us
so high that even angels show respect to us for our lofty position. All
praise is for God because He is "the All-Merciful" and "the All-Compassionate." We find everywhere in the universe the traces of His infinite
mercy, especially in all aspects of our human creation. His Lordship is
manifest everywhere, proving why He deserves all praise.

As God bestows all kinds of blessings upon us, we are responsible
and accountable. He will ask us of all blessings at the end of the day. He
is "the Master of the Day of Judgment." He deserves our praises once
more because He is the unique Owner of that final day. We should be
fully aware of the Final Judgment, which is so hard; but before that, we
should look at the preceding verse, which proclaims: "the All-Merci-

ful" and "the All-Compassionate." This shows that we need to consider the Final Judgment only through or after the consideration of the infinite Divine mercy and compassion. We need to act carefully as required by the Final Judgment, yet we should not be too fearful to live peacefully.

Our contemplations on creation teach us the significance of community. We transcend our personal ego and adopt the collective identity of our community. With this identity, we proclaim, even when we pray privately: "You alone do we worship and from You alone do we seek help." For we understand that we cannot adequately respond to the glory of God Almighty in a private way of worship. An adequate response is possible to some extent only through a communal manner of service. We gather together and stand behind the imam, and consider that all the communities of believers on earth are now combined in a single unity of worship. We even imagine all past generations included in this grand unity standing before the One God. Then we imagine all Prophets along with their respective communities, thinking that we altogether stand behind the Imam, the most perfect Guide and universal Leader of humanity, forming countless rows around the Ka'ba. We altogether proclaim: "You alone do we worship and from You alone do we seek help." Moving one step further, we imagine all members of the universe joining this magnificent congregation to proclaim the same truth.

The harmonious flow of these verses simply charms us. Nothing is missing or needless in this harmony. As we have arrived at a spiritual peak, we passionately ask God: "Guide us to the straight path." For guidance is the most important matter of help. We ask God to bring us to the path which He is pleased with and which all of His Messengers and eminent friends have passed through. At the peak of our spiritual closeness to the Lord of the worlds, we have a little time to ask Him for something, and we ask for the best thing: guidance to the path that leads to Himself eternally.

We ask for guidance, for we are at a crossroads between the right path and the wrong path. We passionately pray: "O God, we want Your path, the path of all Your Messengers. It is the manifest, broadest and safest path, which has been experienced by the best ones of humanity for ages and ages. Recently, Your beloved Apostle, peace and blessings be upon him, proceeded through this path and he managed to establish the foundations of the greatest civilization ever with the help of his truthful companions. This path safely brings its travelers to Your presence, whereas other roads will not lead to Your good pleasure. For there can be only one straight line between two points. Only Your path is straight and all others are curved more or less. We ask You to guide us to the straight path, not others even if they are close to be straight."

O God, help us make the Qur'an the purpose of our lives. Help us make it the life of our lives. *Amin.*

Bibliography

Abd ar-Razzaq, Abu Bakr ibn Hammam, *Al-Musannaf*. Beirut: Al-Maktaba al-Isla-mi, 1983.

Ahmad ibn Hanbal, *Al-Musnad*. Egypt: Muassasa Qurtuba, undated.

Alusi, *Ruh al-Ma'ani*. Beirut: Dar Ihya' at-Turath al-Arabi, undated.

Bayhaqi, *Dalail an-Nubuwwa*. Beirut: Dar al-Kutub al-Ilmiyya, 1985.

_____ *As-Sunan al-Kubra*. Mecca, 1994.

Bukhari, *Sahih*. Istanbul: al-Maktaba al-Islamiyya, 1979.

Jurjani, as-Sayyid ash-Sharif, *At-Ta'rifat*. Beirut: Dar al-Kitab al-Arabi, 1985.

Daraqutni, *Sunan*. Beirut: Dar al-Ma'rifa, 1966.

Darimi, *Sunan*. Beirut: Dar al-Kitab al-Arabi, 1978.

Daylami, *Al-Musnad al-Firdaws*. Beirut: Dar al-Kutub al-Ilmiyya, 1986.

Abu Dawud, *Sunan*. Istanbul: Çağrı, 1992.

Abu Hayyan al-Andalusi, *Al-Bahr al-Muhit*. Dar al-Kutub al-Ilmiyya, 2001.

Abu Nu'aym, *Hilya al-Awliya*. Beirut: Dar al-Kitab al-Arabi, 1985.

Abu Ya'la al-Mawsili at-Tamimi, *Al-Musnad*. Damascus: Dar al-Ma'mun li at-Turath, 1984.

Ghazali, Abu Hamid, *Ihya 'Ulum ad-Din*. Beirut: Dar al-Ma'rifa, undated.

_____ *Al-Maqsad al-Asna*. Cyprus, 1987.

Hakim an-Nisaburi, *Al-Mustadrak*. Beirut: Dar al-Kutub al-Ilmiyya, 1990.

Halabi, Ali ibn Burhan ad-Din, *Insan al-'Uyun*. Beirut: Dar al-Ma'rifa, 1980.

Khatib al-Baghdadi, *Tarikh Baghdad*. Beirut: Dar al-Kutub al-Ilmiyya, undated.

Ibn Abd al-Barr, *Al-Isti'ab fi Ma'rifa al-Ashab*. Beirut: Dar al-Jil, 1992.

Ibn Asakir, *Tarikh Dimashq*. Beirut: Dar al-Fikr, 1986.

Ibn Abi Hatim, *Tafsir al-Qur'an*. Lebanon: Maktaba al-Asriyya, undated.

Ibn Abi Shayba, *Al-Musannaf*. Riyadh: Maktaba ar-Rush, 1989.

Ibn Hibban, *Sahih*. Beirut: Muassasa ar-Risala, 1993.

Ibn Kathir, *Al-Bidaya wa an-Nihaya*. Beirut: Maktaba al-Ma'arif, undated.

Ibn Majah, *Sunan*. Istanbul: Çağrı, 1992.

Ibn Sa'd, *At-Tabaqat al-Kubra*. Beirut: Dar Sadir, undated.

Kalabazi, *At-Ta'arruf*. Beirut: Dar al-Kutub al-Ilmiyya, 1980.

Malik ibn Anas, *Al-Muwatta*. Beirut: Dar Ihya' at-Turath al-Arabi, 1985.

Munawi, *Fayd al-Qadir*. Egypt: Al-Maktaba at-Tijariyya al-Kubra, 1937.

Muslim, *Sahih*. Beirut: Dar ihya' at-Turath al-Arabi, undated.

Nasai, *Sunan*. Istanbul: Çağrı, 1992.

Razi, Fakhruddin, *Mafatih al-Ghayb*. Beirut: Dar al-Kutub al-Ilmiyya, 2000.

Sahavi, *Al-Maqasid al-Hasana*. Beirut: Dar al-Kitab al-Arabi, 1985.

Suyuti, *Ad-Durr al-Manthur*. Beirut: Dar al-Fikr, 1993.

_____ *Sharh Sunan Ibn Majah*. Karachi, undated.

_____ *Ad-Durar al-Muntathira*. Beirut: Maktaba al-Mishkat al-Islamiyya, undated.

Tabarani, *Al-Mu'jam al-Awsat*. Cairo: Dar al-Haramayn, 1995.

_____ *Al-Mu'jam al-Kabir*. Mosul: Maktaba al-Zahra, 1983.

_____ *Musnad ash-Shamiyyin*. Beirut: Muassasa ar-Risala, 1983.

Tabari, *Jami' al-Bayan*. Beirut: Dar al-Fikr, 1985.

Tirmidhi, *Sahih*. Istanbul: Çağrı, 1992.

Zarkashi, *Al-Burhan fi 'Ulum al-Qur'an*. Beirut: Dar al-Ma'rifa, 1970.

Zurqani, *Manahil Al-'Irfan fi 'Ulum al-Qur'an*. Beirut: Dar al-Fikr, 1996.